7 Paths to God

❋   ❋   ❋

BOOKS, AUDIOCASSETTES, AND PROGRAMS BY JOAN BORYSENKO, PH.D.

BOOKS

Minding the Body, Mending the Mind (basic meditation and psychological healing practices), Bantam Books, 1987.

Guilt Is the Teacher, Love Is the Lesson (healing the wounds of childhood and orienting to the Spiritual Self), Warner Books, 1990.

On Wings of Light: Meditations for Awakening to the Source; co-created with artist Joan Drescher, Warner Books, 1992. (Magnificent illustrations and meditations for humans from 6 to 106). There is also an audiocassette version of *On Wings of Light,* narrated by Joan, with an original soundtrack.

Fire in the Soul: A New Psychology of Spiritual Optimism, Warner Books, 1993. (A book for anyone going through crisis, grieving, or wondering about the age-old question of why suffering exists in a loving Universe). *Pocketful of Miracles,* Warner Books, 1995. (A book of daily spiritual practice, prayer, and inspiration.)

The Power of the Mind to Heal, with Miroslav Borysenko, Hay House, 1995. (An update on the connection between mind/body and spirit.)

A Woman's Book of Life: The Biology, Psychology and Spirituality of the Feminine Lifecyle, Riverhead Books, 1996. (How women continue to grow in wisdom, intuition, and the power to change society throughout the lifecycle.)

AUDIOCASSETTE PROGRAMS

Hay House Tapes

- Meditations for Relaxation and Stress Reduction
- Meditations for Self-Healing and Inner Power
- Meditations for Healing the Inner Child and Improving Relationships (for women)

- Meditation on: Invocation of the Angels
- Meditation on: Overcoming Depression
- Meditation on: Lovingkindness and Compassion
- Morning and Evening Prayers and Meditations
- Reflections on *A Woman's Book of Life* (one-hour lecture on side 1; women's wisdom meditation on side 2)
- *Minding the Body, Mending the Mind* (Joan reads her classic *New York Times* bestseller, 4-tape set).
- *The Ways of the Mystic: Seven Paths to God* (Joan reads this book)

OTHER AUDIOCASSETTE PROGRAMS

- *The Power of the Mind to Heal*; Nightingale-Conant, 1993. Six double-sided cassettes that provide up-to-date medical and psychological knowledge about healing, enhanced by wisdom from the world's great spiritual traditions. The set includes several guided meditations and a set of inspiring prayer cards.

- *Seventy Times Seven: On the Spiritual Art of Forgiveness*; Sounds True, 1996. (A three-hour program featuring wisdom and meditations drawn from Jewish, Christian, Taoist, and Native American traditions.)

SPECIAL PROGRAMS

- Weekend spiritual retreats for women—locations around the country
- Lectures, workshops, and five-day training programs on mind/body health for hospitals, health professionals, therapists, and the general public
- Corporate trainings on creativity, stress management, and health
- Spiritual getaways to sacred sites around the world
- Inspirational talks and lectures at conferences, civic and religious organizations

For information or an itinerary, contact: Mind/Body Health Sciences, Inc., 393 Dixon Rd., Boulder, CO 80302 • (303) 440-8460

Please visit the Hay House Website at: **www.hayhouse.com**

7 Paths to God
The Ways of the Mystic

Joan Borysenko, Ph.D.

Hay House, Inc.
Carlsbad, California • Sydney, Australia

Copyright © 1997 by Joan Borysenko

Published and distributed in the United States by:
Hay House, Inc., P.O. Box 5100, Carlsbad, CA 92018-5100
(800) 654-5126 • (800) 650-5115 (fax)

Edited by: Jill Kramer   *Designed by:* Jenny Richards

Unseen Rain: Quatrains of Rumi (1986), translated by John Moyne and Coleman Barks. Reprinted by permission of Threshold Books, 139 Main St., Brattleboro, VT 05301.

The Library of Congress has catalogued this book under the original title of the hardcover edition *(The Ways of the Mystic)*.

Library of Congress Cataloging-in-Publication Data

Borysenko, Joan.
    The ways of the mystic : seven paths to God / Joan Borysenko.
       p.   cm.
    Includes bibliographical references.
    ISBN 1-56170-392-3 (hardcover) • ISBN 1-56170-610-8 (tradepaper)
    1. Mysticism. 2. Spiritual life. I. Title.
BL625.B673   1997
291.4'22--dc21   97-37757
                                   CIP

ISBN 1-56170-610-8

04 03 02 01   9 8 7 6
1st printing, August 2000
6th printing, January 2001

Printed in the United States of America

For my husband, Kurt Kaltreider, Ph.D.,
a Path-One mystic who "Looks With Wonder"

❧ CONTENTS

❋ Acknowledgments

eartfelt thanks to Reid Tracy at Hay House, whose faith in me and commitment to a vision of healing and spirituality has made this book, and countless other projects, possible. You really are an angel, Reid, and a blessing in my life. Thanks, too, to my editor at Hay House, Jill Kramer; and to art director Christy Salinas for capturing the essence of this book in the cover. Thanks, too, to Louise Hay, whose generosity of spirit has offered hope and healing to so many people.

I am forever grateful to my wonderful assistant and steadfast support, Judy Dawson, who kept the world at bay with consistent good cheer while I dropped out of sight to write; my husband, Kurt Kaltreider, whose outrageous sense of humor and steady presence kept me down to earth; dear friend Celia Thaxter Hubbard, my spiritual sounding board; Elizabeth Lawrence and Janet Quinn, both dear friends and partners in women's retreats; Dik Darnell, whose Lakota wisdom, music, and friendship have been a Godsend; Ken Cohen, whose knowledge of Chinese medicine and philosophy have been so enriching;

and Caroline Myss and Mona Lisa Schulz, whose teachings on the chakras have added new psychological depth to ancient yoga science, and whose friendship is much cherished.

I am blessed by a warm and wise circle of friends whose wisdom has enriched these pages: Robin Casarjian, Caroline Ashley, Eve Ilsen and Rabbi Zalman Shachter-Shalomi, Christine and David Hibbard, Reverend Wayne Muller, Naomi Judd, Loretta LaRoche, Rabbi David Cooper and Shoshanna Cooper, Ursula Reich and Alan Shackelford, Rima Laurie, Steve Maurer, and Olivia Hoblitzelle. And to those people who have shared their stories with me and allowed me to share them, in turn, with others, may the blessing you gave return multiplied by all.

❊ INTRODUCTION

From Alone to All One
The Experience of Union

There are moments in life that are watersheds, points of no return, when one's view of the cosmos is forever changed. At the moment of my mother's death, I had a remarkable vision in which I was simultaneously a pregnant mother giving birth and also the baby being born. My mind was present in two bodies, experiencing two different realities, until suddenly I was just the child, sliding down a long, dark tunnel and then emerging into a light of tender mercy and perfect love. The circle of life with my mother was completed in a state of grace. She had borne me physically into this world, and I felt as though I had delivered her soul back into the divine light, being born again myself in the process, for I was no longer the same person. I had met God and remembered the unity of all things, experiencing life as a precious gift that enables us to grow in love and wisdom.

I had read numerous accounts of entering the divine light written by Western and Eastern mystics. And as director of a Mind/Body Clinic at one of the Harvard Medical School teaching hospitals for most of the 1980s, I had also heard hundreds of near-death experiences and deathbed visions in which people reported leaving their bodies, traveling down tunnels or across vast spaces, and finally meeting the light. But reading or hearing about such an experience is very different from having one, simply because they are indescribable even in metaphor, the language of Spirit.

> *How can words convey the depth and sweetness of unconditional love, the soul's joy in coming home to God, the stunning revelation that despite all your errors you are forgiven? How to describe the realization that your every thought and deed is known, and the bliss of being shown that your soul is pure, not because you are perfect, but because you are willing to acknowledge your imperfections? How is it possible that you can think about anything and know instantly, at an infinite number of levels, its very essence? How to convey the perception that everything is interconnected, crafted of an intelligent light that forms a seamless matrix from which all matter springs?*

Gallup polls indicate that 5 percent of Americans have had a near-death experience. Most of those have entered the light. Many others, like me, have had light experiences without being near death. The Catholic priest, sociologist, and novelist, Andrew Greeley, calls America a nation of closet mystics. In the last ten years, we have started coming out of the closet. Movies about angels, life after death, and God are increasingly popular, as are television programs and books. While some people define interest in such things as New Age, mystical experiences have been reported in every religious tradition for thousands of years. They are more Old Age than New Age. Consider the conversion of St. Paul.

Early in the history of Christianity, a man named Saul was intent on stamping out the new Jewish sect. Marching resolutely down the road to Damascus, Saul was flooded by heavenly light, which literally knocked him off his feet. The young zealot heard the voice of Jesus asking, "Saul, Saul, why do you persecute me?"[1] Struck blind, Saul was instructed to rise and enter Damascus, where he would be told what to do. For three days and nights, he neither ate nor drank, moved to intense prayer and meditation. He was then visited by a man called Ananais, a healer who had been instructed by Jesus in a vision to lay on hands and heal Saul from his blindness so that he could undertake his divine mission. Ananais argued with Jesus that Saul was a nasty piece of work, not worth healing. Jesus knew better. We are all worth healing. Furthermore, Saul's background as a skeptic made him the ideal person to bring Jesus' teachings to the Greeks and Romans.

The transformation of Saul the sinner into Paul the

saint is an archetype—a cosmic blueprint—of grace in action. Most of us don't get stopped in our tracks in the dramatic way Paul did, but we have all had holy moments, experiences in which time seems to stop and our senses become preternaturally sharp. Everything seems brighter and more beautiful, as the normally busy mind slows down and savors the present. These moments, the memory of which often accompanies us for a lifetime, can strike anytime, anywhere.

At a conference where I was lecturing, an elderly couple stepped into the crowded elevator. The gentleness of the wife's hand on her husband's shoulder as she guided him in, and the innocent sweetness with which her eyes swept over the ten or so of us fellow travelers, invited me into a holy moment. I felt as if I were in her skin, a proud grandmother casting her net of love over a brood of strangers that somehow were all her children and grandchildren. My heart overflowed with the joy in her heart, and for a moment we were one.

When the heart is open, we overcome the illusion that we are separate from one another, and the mystery of divine love wraps us in a cloak of security, unity, wisdom, and joy. All is right with the world. We are mystics because we have seen the face of the Mystery, the great paradox. Everything seems separate, yet we have just experienced oneness. Albert Einstein once remarked that the illusion that we are separate is an optical delusion of consciousness. Indeed, in holy moments we are aware that there is only One Mind in the universe, a Mind present in every thing and every one.

> *A mystic sees beyond the illusion of separateness into the intricate web of life in which all things are expressions of a single Whole. You can call this web God, the Tao, the Great Spirit, the Infinite Mystery, Mother or Father, but it can be known only as love.*

In the Judeo-Christian tradition, the shift of perception from isolation to unity has been labeled a conversion experience. Conversion means turning around, changing our point of view so that we see with God's eyes, the eyes of the heart, like St. Paul. Instead of feeling *alone*, we become *all one*. A Course in Miracles calls this the atonement, or *at-one-ment*. The miracle that the Course speaks of is the change in perception that Buddhists would call an awareness of one's own true nature. Every religion has its own words to describe the conversion—the miracle of seeing with the eyes of the heart.

Commandments such as the Golden Rule: *"Do unto others as you would have them do unto you,"* take on a deeper meaning when we understand that whatever we do to another, we automatically do to ourselves. The primary prayer of the Jewish tradition is "Hear, Oh Israel, the Lord our God the Lord is One." In this prayer, Israel does not refer to a state in the sense of a piece of land. It refers to a state of consciousness, and means literally, "One who wrestles with God"—in other words, one who seeks to experience the mystery. It is a reminder of the mystical core of every religion: *We are one.*

> *He is one, the lord and innermost Self of all;*
> *of one form, he makes of himself many forms.*
> *To him who sees the Self revealed in his*
> *own heart belongs eternal bliss.*
> — Katha Upanishad, Ancient India[2]

> *My teachings are older than the world.*
> *How can you grasp their meaning?*
> *If you want to know me, look inside your heart.*
> — Tao Te Ching, Ancient China[3]

> *One must know that no existing thing has*
> *an independent existence.*
> *One must know that all things are interdependent.*
> — *Precepts of the Gurus,* Tibetan Buddhist Text[4]

> *I and my father are one...understand that the*
> *Father is in me and I am in the Father.*
> — Jesus, John 10:30, 38

And your God is one God, there is no God but
The One, the Compassionate, the Merciful.
— The Koran, Surah 2

Everyone is sacred. You're sacred and I'm
sacred. Every time you blink your eye, or I blink
my eye, God blinks His eye. God sees through
your eyes and my eyes.
We are sacred.
— Mathew King, Chief Noble Red Man, Lakota[5]

The word *conversion* is often applied to the acceptance of a particular religious dogma, when in fact, it transcends all dogmas, referring to the direct perception of unity and the realization that everything is sacred. All religions lead to God, just the way that all rivers empty into the sea. Dogma is less important than passion, the heartfelt longing for divine union that motivates an intense search for God. God doesn't mind if you come by land or sea, on foot or by train, through the appreciation of beauty or the dedication of your life to others. It doesn't matter if you join a monastery or an ashram, or if you prefer the life of a householder.

Different religions and paths to God suit different personality types. Some of us relate to God best through the intellect, others through the emotions. Some crave ritual; others thrive on simplicity. Hasidic Jews and Sufi (Islamic) dervishes relate to God as the Beloved, and enter the state of unity through joyful singing and dance. Native Americans and other First Nations People find God through nature and community, prayer and ceremony. Christians, who comprise 500 diverse sects, may find God through intellect, ritual, song, service, grace, prayer, or the transubstantiation of bread and wine into the body and blood of Jesus. Buddhists find enlightenment through discipline of the mind, the precepts of right living, meditation, prayer, and the practice of compassion. The 13th-century Islamic poet–saint, Jelalluddin Rumi, wrote:

> *Sometimes visible, sometimes not, sometimes*
> *devout Christians, sometimes staunchly Jewish.*
> *Until our inner love fits into everyone,*
> *all we can do is take daily these different shapes.*[6]

The great philosopher William James noted that the miracle of conversion, the opening of the heart to cosmic consciousness, can occur in two ways—suddenly through crisis, or gradually through lysis. These are akin to a shoreline changing almost instantly through volcanic eruption, or more slowly through the inevitable working of the tides. In studying the world's spiritual traditions and hearing the personal stories of people's search for God, it has become clear that the saying, "Different strokes for different folks," is as true for people's spirituality as it is for their diets and their love lives. Unfortunately, many of us have been taught that there is only one path to God, and that those who don't follow it are either damned to Hell or doomed to lose their souls. Some of my relatives who are Jehovah's Witnesses sincerely anguish over my unwillingness to recognize their religion as the only true Way, since they believe that my soul will cease to exist after the Judgment, and I will be permanently lost to them. While I admire their devotion to God, service, and community, I am also saddened by their denial of other paths.

In this book, I have distilled seven different paths to divine union that the Great Mysterious, as the Lakota call the Creator, has hardwired into our bodymind. The paths that you will read about in the next chapter correspond to the ancient notion of sacred sevens. Just as the unity of white light is divisible into the seven colors of the spectrum, and the lifeforce energy is distributed through the body by seven chakras or energy transformers, the Native Americans recognize the different energies of the seven sacred directions. These paths are spiritual rather than religious. Whether you are devoted to a particular religion or not, it is my hope that these paths will provide a framework for different paths to God that you will find validating and encouraging.

— Joan Borysenko
Gold Hill, Colorado
July, 1999

❋ CHAPTER ONE

The Rainbow Bridge
Seven Paths to God

The rainbow has long been a symbol of hope, as white light passes through prisms of raindrops, and seven distinct colors are revealed. I think of the rainbow as a metaphor for the seven paths to God, which are likewise a part of what seems to be an indivisible whole—each a precious reflection of one aspect of divine consciousness. The pot of gold at the end of the rainbow is our relationship to God; happiness, gratitude, and the knowledge that we have been given unique gifts with which to serve.

The number seven has special properties in most ancient traditions. Religious historian Rosemarie Schimmel documents numerous references to the number seven in both the natural and supernatural worlds:[1] seven seas and seven heavens, seven planets of the solar system, seven days of the week, and seven notes to the musical scale. Creation was fashioned in seven days—including the Sabbath, or day of rest. Seven steps led to Solomon's temple, which was built in seven years. The Proverbs extol the Seven Pillars of Wisdom, and throughout the Old Testament, seven recurs as a power number. In the New Testament, Jesus prescribes that we forgive 70 times 7. In the Book of Revelation, Christ held seven stars in his hand, seven seals are opened, letters are sent to the seven churches, seven trumpets announce the Judgment Day, and seven angels pour out seven bowls of tribulation. There are seven sacraments, seven deadly sins, and seven charisms, or gifts of spirit.

There are seven branches to the Tree of Life in Kabbalistic Judaism. Sufism, the mystical aspect of Islam, states that the mind of God unfolds into the human intellect in a seven-step process. The Buddha sought enlightenment for seven years and circled the Bodhi tree seven times before settling beneath it for his final meditation prior to enlightenment. Hinduism is also based on a system of sevens, including a medical/philosophical understanding of the lifeforce energy, or *prana*, that powers the human body. Prana circulates in *nadis*, similar to acupuncture meridians, that flow into seven wheels of energy called *chakras.*

In the tradition of the Native American Medicine Wheel, there are seven sacred directions. Beneath our feet is Mother or Grandmother Earth. Above us is Father or Grandfather Sky, the direction of Wakan Tanka, the Great Sacred Mystery. To the East lies the power of the rising sun. To the South lies abundance and creativity. To the

West lies transformation. To the North lies wisdom. The seventh direction, where all energies come together, is within our heart.

In this book, we will consider how the seven directions and the seven chakras reveal seven paths to God. Although we will discuss these paths in a sequence that may seem linear, one path is no more "advanced" than another. They are simply different expressions, distinct rays of energy that each of us embody. But before we examine the different paths on the spiritual spectrum, let us turn to white light—the universal energy—from which they spring.

Light: The Energy of Creation

God's first creation in the book of Genesis was light. Many mystical accounts involve light or luminosity, which may culminate in union with God, a realization of the unity of all things, or a prophetic vision. The Hebrew prophet Ezekiel was absorbed in a glowing cloud of fire that contained a luminous crystalline vault, guarded by winged creatures, half man and half beast. He emerged with a prophecy concerning the destruction of Jerusalem. The first century Rabbi Akiva ascended through the seven heavens and the seven palaces in the highest heaven by means of passwords uttered to the angelic gatekeepers. His meetings with God were again characterized by luminosity. St. Paul was blinded by a flash of heavenly light on the road to Damascus and was transformed from a persecutor of Christians into a servant of Christ. Near-death experiencers, a diverse group of modern-day mystics from every religion, also speak of meeting with a divine light that changes their lives and tutors them on the interconnectedness of all things.

When I accompanied my mother into the light at her time of death, the light accompanied me back into the everyday world. When I opened my eyes, everything in the hospital room seemed made of light. The floor, the air, the bed on which the empty physical shell of my mother lay, and the very living body of my son, who had also been keeping the deathbed vigil for his grandmother, was glowing. Everything was interconnected, densities in a luminous whole. My son, his face filled with awe, tears streaming from his eyes, announced in hushed tones that the room was filled with light. He asked if I could see it, too. When I nodded that I could, he whispered that it was his grandmother's last gift to us, that she was holding open the door to eternity so that we could have a glimpse.

For the most part, the divine light is hidden. Occasionally, through grace, the door to eternity does open, and we catch a tiny glimpse of the inexpressible beauty of creation. But in its most basic sense, the light is always with us. It is the lifeforce itself. Through it, flowers grow, humans and animals live, and the universe continually evolves. The lifeforce that enlivens living things is recognized by 49 cultures around the world and is intimately related to physical health and healing. Western culture, however, has no name for it or framework for its action. Chinese call this lifeforce energy *chi*, the Japanese *ki*, the Hindus *prana*.

One of the best known systems of lifeforce energy comes from yoga science, which identifies 72,000 subtle channels, or *nadis*, in the human body through which prana circulates. These channels of energy flow into a major river, the *susumna*, which travels the length of the spinal cord, and comprises two main branches. The right nadi, called the *Pingala,* is also know as *Surya-Nadi*. It is the channel for male energy, *Surya,* meaning "sun." It generates heat and is reminiscent of the Chinese concept of *yang,* or dry, hot, active male energy. The left, or female nadi, is called *Chandra-Nadi. Chandra* means "moon," and its energy is cool, receptive, and passive,[2] similar to the Chinese concept of female *yin* energy. The balance of these energies is thought to be critical for health, well-being, creativity, and God-Union. *When the male and female energies come to balance, the latent energy at the base of the spine, called kundalini, shoots up the susumna, opens the chakras, and delivers the individual to God-Union, which is the actual meaning of yoga.*

The energies of Ida and Pingala flow through, and are balanced by a number of transformers, the chakras, which literally mean "wheels." The activity of these wheels is related to many different inputs: the quality of breathing, food choice, constitution, time in nature, prayer, meditation, attitude about life, and various psychological issues. Yoga researchers have correlated the seven chakras with specific nerve plexuses, endocrine glands, and medical conditions that relate to disturbances in nervous system and glandular activity when chakras are blocked, creating inefficient flow of lifeforce energy.

A number of contemporary Western healers and researchers work with the chakra system. Annodea Judith is a therapist who has researched ancient yoga principles and was one of the first to distill them into a cohesive spiritual, psychological, and physical healing system. Barbara Ann Brennan is a former NASA research scientist who is also a healer, teacher, scientist, and psychotherapist working with the human energy system and the chakras. Caroline Myss, Ph.D., is a theologian and medical intuitive. She wrote *Anatomy of the Spirit: The Seven Stages of Power and Healing,* which is a brilliant synthesis of the material on the chakras, the seven sacraments of Catholicism, the seven branches of the Kabbalistic Tree of Life, and the different ways that people heal emotionally and spiritually.

In organizing the seven paths to God, I have drawn on the accounts of mystics from many traditions, on ancient yoga science, on contemporary work on the chakras, and on the seven directions of the Native American Medicine Wheel. The impersonal energy of each direction is personalized in our bodies through the chakras, allowing us to respond to the cycles and seasons—to the use of energy that they represent. A brief summary of this correlation follows.

Path One—Earth and Home: The Everyday Mystic

Path One corresponds to the color red, the blood of the womb of our physical mother, and to the fiery womb at the core of Grandmother Earth who nourishes us all. In the tradition of the Medicine Wheel, it represents the Earth, the direction *Down*. In the language of yoga, Path One flows from the root chakra, the place where the lifeforce energy is curled like a serpent, waiting to unfold the creative process of life.

Path One is earth-centered, home-centered. It is the domain of what I call the everyday mystic, who sees the Creator in every bush and tree, in the gifts of food and shelter, in nurturing and in the fulfillment of the everyday needs of life. It is the path of gratitude and caretaking of the earth and all her creatures. The Path-One mystic embodies a trusting, powerful, earth-centered spirituality like that of First Nations People, including the Native Americans. Their tribes had a strong sense of place and a history rooted in a particular geographical area. At one with the physical world around them, they perceived the interconnectedness of all things, the circular nature of the universe, and the rightness of both birth and death in the overall scheme of creation.

Path Two—Creativity and Abundance: Generosity of Spirit

Path Two follows the direction *South* on the Medicine Wheel, the summer season of increase and abundance when the earth bears fruit. This seasonal energy is related to the personal energy of the second chakra: sexuality and birth. Yoga science relates the creative second chakra to the Leydig cells that occur both in the ovaries and the testes. These cells synthesize testosterone and mediate our ability to carve out territory for ourselves, a niche in which we will bring forth the abundance of our soul, offering our gifts to the world.

In this path of creativity and abundance, male and female aspects join. Our male aspect provides the space in which our feminine aspect becomes the womb of creativity. In the Hindu tradition, this is called *tantra yoga*, the sacred marriage of male and female. The eight books I have authored, the mind/body program I helped develop, and the students I have mentored are the fruits of combining my male and female aspects. Offering these gifts to the world is pure joy, and the energy that comes back to me from those who receive them keeps the creativity flowing. The key to Path Two is generosity of spirit—being secure enough in ourselves that we can receive from God and give to others in a way that encourages both of us to bring forth our creative gifts.

Path Three—How Can I Help?: The Passion to Serve

The third path follows the direction *East* on the Medicine Wheel, the spring season when the lifeforce returns after winter. In yoga science, this seasonal energy is carried personally within our solar plexus or adrenal center. East is the direction of the rising sun, the new day that brings the energy and power to dream a new world into being. Similarly, the third chakra is the powerhouse of action, the furnace of passion and emotion whose fire fuels our dreams and gives us the stamina to fulfill them. Think of Biblical prophets such as fiery Elijah, feisty martyrs such as Joan of Arc, or modern orators and visionaries such as Martin Luther King. These charismatic people emanate a kind of "fire in the belly," an undeniable passion that can either make people sit up and take notice or run for cover.

The basic question for Path-Three mystics is: "Whom do I serve?" If we serve ourselves, to the exclusion of others, as do dictators and power-hungry zealots such as Hitler, we fall into spiritual peril and are likely to add chaos, rather than creativity, to the universe. If we serve the world, we use our potential as co-creators with God. Path Three is what the Hindus call *karma yoga*, the path to God-Union through service.

Path Four—The Way of the Heart:
Bridging Earth and Heaven

The fourth path follows the seventh direction of the Medicine Wheel: *Within*, and the fourth chakra, the heart or thymus center. The Path-Four mystic can truly say, "I love the Lord My God with all my heart, soul, and mind, and I love my neighbor as myself." The Hindus call this path *bhakti yoga*, the way of devotion. One may be devoted to a personal aspect of God such as Krishna, Jesus, Buddha, or the Mother Mary—or to the realization that, when we see with the eyes of the heart, we can worship God within every person.

Yoga research correlates the heart chakra with the cardiac plexus and the thymus gland. The thymus is an organ of the immune system, and the cells that develop within it are called T-cells. The job of the immune system is to tell self from not-self. It is a boundary organ. In Eastern thought, the thymus regulates the boundary between earth and heaven. The heart chakra is the midpoint between the three lower and three higher energy wheels. It is represented in *Hindu* iconography by the six-pointed star, which in Judaism is the Star of David, or Solomon's Seal. It symbolizes the downward ray of God's energy, which meets the upward ray of human energy. The heart chakra is thus considered the meeting point of earth and heaven, karma and grace. Path-Four mystics such as Mother Teresa bring about heaven on earth through love.

Path Five—Discipline, Ethics and Will: Thy Will, Not Mine, Be Done

The fifth path follows the direction *North* on the Medicine Wheel, the season of winter in which stories are told and we reflect on the natural order of the universe and our place within it. This impersonal energy of order is reflected personally in the fifth chakra, the throat or thyroid center that represents discipline, will, and responsibility. In Hindu philosophy, this is the path of *raja yoga*— God-Union by following the specific moral disciplines that preserve the community, honor life, and lead to personal growth. For the observant Jew, it means carrying out the letter of the law as prescribed in the Torah and the Talmud, with one's whole heart and mind.

The Ten Commandments, like the Buddhist precepts for living and the Hindu system of raja yoga, provide a template for using our human will to live in accordance with the divine will. Those who take such commandments to heart struggle with moral dilemmas: Is war ever righteous since it violates the commandment against killing? Is abortion a sin, and is it any less of a sin to bomb an abortion clinic to stop it? Many Path-Five mystics walk a narrow line between obedience to God and blind zealotry. Like St. Paul, they can be dangerous when doing their own will, but inspired and inspiring when doing God's will. The bottom line for Path Five mystics is whether their acts are kind and compassionate—not in the abstract, but in the particular moment—and for the particular person with whom they are interacting.

Path Six—Opening the Wisdom Eye:
Contemplation and Transformation

The sixth path follows the direction *West* on the Medicine Wheel, the fall season when the lifeforce energy withdraws and nature goes to sleep. The abode of the setting sun, west is the direction of the ego death that makes room for rebirth into spirit. This is often accomplished by undergoing a dark night of the soul, like the Buddha, when our old life is left behind and we enter a period of wandering or searching before the sun of enlightenment rises. When we awaken to our new life, we see things not through our physical eyes, but through the wisdom eye. As Jesus said, "Your eye is the lamp of your body; when your eye is sound, your whole body is full of light; but when it is not sound, your body is full of darkness."[3]

Yoga science relates the sixth chakra to the pineal gland, a vestigial third eye complete with light receptors, which the French philosopher René Descartes called the "seat of the soul." It has long been linked with higher intuition, "medicine," or teaching dreams and visions. The dark night of transformation calls out the question: "Who am I? Am I just this body, or I am something more?" In answering this question, the Path-Six mystic is called to deep meditation and contemplation. These practices help her to shed the ego's attachments to praise and blame, tragedy and triumph. Through them she develops the contentment, equanimity, and compassion of one who has communed with God and knows the beauty of life, beyond the appearances of suffering and limitation. In the Hindu system, Path Six corresponds to *jnana yoga*, the path of insight.

Path Seven—The Way of Faith: Paradox and Grace

The seventh path follows the direction *Above* in the Medicine Wheel, representing the action of Wakan Tanka, the Great Sacred, or the Great Spirit, as it is often translated. In yoga science, it correlates with the seventh, or crown chakra, where the lifeforce energy enters the body and God becomes manifest in physical form. Our faith is an important determiner of openness to Spirit. The nature of our faith develops and changes throughout the lifecycle, through the dark nights of the soul when we are challenged to transform, and through the work we do on the different spiritual paths. Eventually we have the faith to recognize that grace is a paradox; apparently wonderful events can curb our growth, while devastating events may spur it. We then receive the higher grace of nonattachment.

If we follow our spiritual path and do the required psychological healing along the way, we set the stage for God-

Union. But we will never get there through works, for ultimately, God-Union is a grace, the unearned gift of a generous parent to her child. Whether it occurs while we are
in this body or when we have been reborn to the Spirit
World is not important, nor within our control. And since
the state of union is sometimes beyond the capacity of our
perceptions, its truest measure is in the kindness, creativity, charity, and compassion that are the fruits of Spirit
made manifest in our life.

Your Primary and Secondary Path

We are each working with the energy of all seven
directions, all seven chakras, but in my experience each of
us has one primary and one secondary, or supporting, path
on which we concentrate the majority of our energies. *Our
primary path is the one through which our major contribution to the world will be made. It comes naturally to us.*
For instance, Path Two—creativity and abundance—represents my work in the world. My greatest joy is to write and
teach and to help others recognize and use their gifts. I love
to study—as a doctorate, three postdoctoral fellowships at
Harvard Medical School, writing eight books, and being a
lifelong learner—demonstrate. These are natural talents
necessary to fulfill my soul purpose. While I had to develop them, the raw material was already there.

My secondary path relates to the seventh direction,

Within, or the heart chakra. *Our secondary spiritual path is often based on a wound whose healing will develop qualities that we need in support of our primary purpose.* All my life I could easily give love, but for reasons stemming from my childhood, felt unworthy to receive it. So the love I gave was of a limited type, calculated to get people to like me. I had trouble giving people honest feedback about behaviors that hurt me, for fear they would be angry with me. I also had to learn that giving people everything they want may disempower them, rather than helping them bring forth their gifts. In order for me to use my gifts as a Path-Two teacher, I had to learn about love, a process that continues to unfold.

In addition to our primary and secondary paths, we also learn to use the energies of the other paths as they are needed to fulfill our purpose. With time you will recognize how working with the different paths can help you develop skills and attitudes that may not be innate, and which you will need at different times in your life and work.

Suggestions for the Reader

• **Read through the entire book** before you zero in on your primary and secondary paths. Since several paths may have elements that appeal to you, it can take time and reflection to settle on the best fit.

• **Consider trying the practices of the secondary path first,** for a full 28-day cycle. Since this is the path that may correspond to the healing of old wounds, following the suggestions for that path may help free blocked energies and open up new understanding. Your natural, primary path will then be easier to follow. When you feel ready, follow the suggestions that accompany your primary path.

Why follow a 28-day, or lunar cycle? Every seven days the moon enters a new phase. According to Lakota wisdom,[4] each of us is accompanied through life by 48 guardian angels. Twelve are with us at any given time, and the shift changes every seven days with the phases of the moon. In 28 days, then, we have experienced the entire angelic guard assigned to us by Divine Providence, and they all know, and can support, our intentions.

❊ ❊ ❊

✸ CHAPTER TWO

Path One
Earth and Home
The Everyday Mystic

There is an old story about a certain Mrs. Finegold who lives in Brooklyn. She calls the travel agent to book passage to a remote village in Nepal. He's shocked. "Sophie, you have no idea what a schlepp it is to get there. You have to take two planes, a train across the Punjab where there's guerilla warfare, and then go by camel for a week. And there's no kosher food!"

"Never mind," she says. "I've had a revelation and I'm going." So she loads her backpack full of rye bread and hard cheese. After ten days of strenuous travel, Sophie arrives at last in the camp of the great guru only to discover that there's a three-week wait to see him. Seekers have come from all over the world to find the meaning of life, to rid themselves of depression, and to have a profound mystical experience. Furthermore, when her turn comes, she is told that she can say only three words. So, she settles down and waits with great patience. At last, the big moment arrives and they usher her into a cave redolent of incense and twinkling with the lights of a thousand candles. In the back of the cave is a bearded man wearing saffron robes, his eyes half-closed in a state of transcendent bliss. Upon seeing him, Sophie's whole body pulses with recognition, and she is filled with joy. Rushing forward, she grabs him by the shoulders, shakes him back to awareness, and stares straight into his eyes with a look of triumph as she cries: "Morris—come home!"

The point of this pithy Jewish teaching tale is that mystical experience is not necessarily found just in the heights of visionary experience—in monasteries, ashrams, or in living the life of a saint. It is found at home, where we live, in the daily pursuit of our lives. It has been said that the true measure of spirituality lies not in having visions of angels, but in the ability to make that unpleasant phone call. As Sophie might say in Yiddish, spirituality is about being a "mensch," a human being in the fullest sense of the word.

Growing up Jewish, I understood what a mensch was supposed to be, but the very word—which literally means "man"—was disconcerting. Jewish women, at least so far as my girlfriends and I could see, were second-class citizens. We could not be rabbis or a part of minions, groups of ten men required for certain prayers. One of those very prayers, in fact, was a thanksgiving to God for not being born a woman. We asked the rabbi about this prayer, and he sidestepped us, extolling the virtues of women. We were naturally spiritual, he said, because we kept the home, taught the children, and carried out the cycle of Holy Days. Men, who had to work, were out of touch with the natural order and therefore needed special prayers and rituals to reconnect with it.

Hogwash, we thought. Just one more way to justify keeping women barefoot and pregnant.

It took nearly 35 years of studying the world's religions—and living life—to conclude that perhaps the rabbi was not entirely a sexist pig. Even though I have always worked outside the home, I understand the spirituality of being a "kinkeeper," in charge of gathering the clan, preserving the rituals and continuing the cycle of holidays (holy days). Nourishing a family physically, emotionally and spiritually is in itself a spiritual path for either the woman or the man who enters fully into it, whether or not he or she has outside work.

The Earth Is Our Home

What does it mean to fully enter into the path of the householder? My mother kept house beautifully, had no outside work, loved her children, put Herculean effort into the holidays, and worked for charity. But she was not an everyday, earth-centered mystic. The true Path-One mystic lives in accord with what is called in Hebrew, *Ahavat habriot*, the love of all God's creatures and the absolute responsibility for their survival. Like many children, I had no idea that roast beef came from a cow who was a living being. I had no concern for the welfare of cows or gratitude that a sentient creature gave its life so that I could eat. The substantial remains of Sunday's huge roast beef was "fed to the pig," meaning the garbage disposal, by Tuesday because my mother was dreadfully afraid of food poisoning. She cherished the health of her family, but not of the cow.

This type of thinking is called *anthropocentrism*. It places human beings at the center of the universe and everything else becomes peripheral and disposable. We're the King of the Castle, and all else the "dirty rascals." Since all life is interconnected, however, anthropocentric thinking will eventually dirty and dispose of ourselves. How long can chemical fertilizers be used on fields before the earth becomes unproductive? How long can pesticides be sprayed on crops before humans, four-leggeds, birds, and fish die, as well as the bugs? How long can we dump toxic wastes before they leach out and pollute our children and our children's children, gradually destroying life on earth?

Research indicates that approximately 80 percent of cancers come from environmental causes. Preliminary research also shows that the increase in violence, hyperactivity, and learning disabilities in children is probably contributed to by polychlorinated biphenyls, or PCBs, common earth and water pollutants that are byproducts of electrical insulation. When I was teaching medical histology (the study of cells and tissues) at Tufts University Medical School in the mid-1970s, I found data that 50 percent of all nursing mothers had levels of PCBs in their milk that rendered it unfit for human consumption. I can only assume that the situation has deteriorated since that time.

Yet, a mere 150 years ago, vast areas of western America were pristine, populated by many different tribes of First Nation's People, now called Indians. No matter what the tribe, and how their customs and creation stories differed, they had earth-centered spirituality in common. By the 1870s, most of the tribes had been "subdued," their land stolen from them in broken treaties so that it could be used for settlements, cattle grazing, farming, and mining of the prized yellow stone: gold. In December of 1854, the Duwamish Chief Seathl (Seattle) from the Puget Sound area of what is now Washington State gave an impassioned speech in response to the federal government's request to buy the land and put the Indians on a reservation.

Dr. Henry Smith, who spoke the Indian dialect in which the speech was delivered, took notes. The book *How Can One Sell the Air?* is the best-researched reconstruction of Chief Seathl's words. I can only imagine his sadness as he spoke of how the ashes of his people's ancestors were sacred, their graves holy ground, while the white man left the bones of their fathers behind. "Every part of this earth is sacred to my people, every hillside, every valley, every clearing and wood, is holy in the memory and experience of my people."[1]

First Nation's People around the world consider the earth, and their particular location upon the earth, sacred.

Every hill and valley is indeed filled with history and meaning. The Aboriginal people of Australia traveled the continent using song-lines. Elements of the landscape that resembled animals, for example, were woven into a sung story—a spiritual story that instructed the journeyer. When an animal or plant is taken for food in many of these cultures, an apology is made to its spirit. Plants, too, are thanked for their role in the circle of life. In the Lakota tradition, when a plant is harvested, an offering of cornmeal or tobacco is returned to the earth, the source of our nourishment. The earth is not a ball of fire, rock, and soil to be exploited, but the womb of a living, breathing, conscious Mother who births and sustains us all. Whatever we do to the earth, we do to ourselves.

> *The late Mathew King was a contemporary Lakota elder. He said, "God gives His instructions to every creature, according to His plan for the world. He gave his instructions to all the things of nature....Our instructions are very simple—to respect the Earth and each other, to respect life itself. That's our first commandment, the first line of our gospel.*[2]

A primary concept of earth-centered spirituality is to consider every action seven generations into the future. What effect will pesticides sprayed now have in 140 years? Are we mortgaging the future of our children for a quick return? We can all learn important lessons from those who have lived in harmony with the earth from the beginning of time. Ohiyesa, a Plains Indian whose white name was Charles Alexander Eastman, was the first Native American to go to medical school. He wrote a beautiful book called *The Soul of the Indian* in 1911. To the Indian everything has a soul: the rocks, the seven directions, the wind and water, earth and fire, the plants and animals, the sun, and the moon and stars.

Eastman was eloquent about the need for solitude to commune with God in the temple of nature, meeting the Great Mystery not in houses of worship, but "in the mysterious, shadowy aisles of the primeval forest, or on the sun-lit bosom of virgin prairies, upon dizzy spires of naked rock, and yonder in the jeweled vault of the night sky!"[3] The solitary communion with the Unseen, as Eastman often referred to God, was carried out by rising to meet the morning sun, by practicing gratitude for all things, and by seeing all life as sacred. The most important duty to the Indian was prayer, the daily recognition and thanksgiving for life.

Are You an Earth-Centered Mystic?

I live on the edge of a wilderness area in the tiny mountain town of Gold Hill, Colorado. Until the 1860s gold rush, the land on which I live was the summering ground for the Ute Indians. Arrowheads and hidescrapers are easy to find, and the wild winds, awesome views, summer wildflowers, soft winter snows, and the smell of sage and juniper call one into nature. I love the deep silence here. In this arid high desert, not even the sound of a cricket disrupts the velvety silence. I try to live lightly, with as little waste as possible. Recycling is a must. I generally keep track of the phases of the moon, the subtle seasonal changes, and the progression of nature and its effect upon the psyche. I have put down roots here and made a home, but I am not a Path-One mystic.

"Sandra," an acquaintance of mine, is definitely a Path-One mystic. She has raised her children with reverence for the earth. They eat only organic food and take time to honor the spirits of the plants and animals in their meals by saying a meaningful, not a rote, grace, as a family. Although she is a practicing Catholic, Sandra celebrates the solstices and equinoxes, realizing that every religion took the cues for its celebrations from the seasons. For example, to her, all the winter Festivals of Light— Solstice, Christmas, and Hanukkah—honor the return of light and hope.

Sandra is also an environmental activist, and she teaches these principles carefully to her children. She says that it is physically painful for her to see the earth disturbed, and she spontaneously sings healing songs to Grandmother

Earth when she passes construction sites. You won't find an unnecessary light on in Sandra's home because wasting electricity is damaging to the earth. She washes out the plastic bags that she puts vegetables in at the market, because waste of any sort bothers her. *She hasn't so much learned to do these things, as she has responded to a need deep inside of her.* Remember, your primary path is one that comes naturally, from deep within your soul.

Sandra and her family go on camping trips to remote wilderness areas as often as possible. This is where she feels most alive. She thrives on silence and begins most every day at sunrise with a meditative walk and prayers outside. When her parents sold their summer home on a hundred acres in which she had spent so much of her childhood, Sandra cried for months. The land has now been developed into a shopping center and she cannot bring herself to revisit it. Her connection to the earth, to the place where she was raised, to keeping a home that nourishes her family in body, mind and spirit, to the cycles and seasons, to the attitude of gratitude for life in all its great variety— these are the cues to Sandra's Path to God Union.

Suggestions for the Path-One Mystic

1. Practice gratitude. Jews have over 100 *baruchas,* prayers of thanksgiving, for natural blessings: a prayer upon seeing the morning and evening stars, and even a prayer upon moving one's bowels to thank God for making such perfect interior plumbing! The Calmaldolese monk, Brother David Steindl-Rast, suggests being grateful each night for one thing that you have never thought about being grateful for before. This is easy for a month or so, then you have to pay closer attention to life. I have found myself being grateful for the mysterious shadows that leaves cast on the side of a building, for seeing our dog smile, for smelling the first sage of summer, and for a carpenter's level that fell in the garage and gouged a hole beside my eye rather than in it. Gratitude makes you naturally mindful and predisposes you to having holy moments, one of the hallmarks of an everyday mystic.

2. Say grace. Mindless grace parroted by rote doesn't count. The Vietnamese Buddhist monk, peacemaker, and meditation teacher, Thich Nhat Hanh, says a grace of true interconnectedness and respect. Having a plate of pasta and a salad? Think about the fields of wheat and vegetables that grew in the breast of Grandmother Earth, the influence of the sun and moon, and the rain and winds that nourished the plants. What about the farmer and laborers who planted and harvested the wheat? Those who stored and trucked it. The millers and packagers. The pasta makers. The supermarket workers. The person who prepared the meal. The God who created your wondrous body, ready to receive the nourishment. Those who will share it with you and those who may have nothing to eat. Blessed be all life.

3. Protect the earth. Buy natural, organic foods, including dairy products and meat if you eat it. The latter two items are the most concentrated source of toxins since they are high in fat, and most of the poisons that find their way into the food chain are fat soluble. Choose items with as little packaging as possible. Buy in bulk and bring your own containers. Buy canvas bags to take to the supermarket— they last for years. Do not use commercial lawn foods, pesticides, herbicides, or fertilizers around your house. There are natural, nontoxic alternatives. Lobby local schools to do the same. Turn the lights, stereo, and television off when you leave the room. In winter, keep the house five degrees cooler and wear a sweater. In summer, save air conditioning if you use it by keeping the house five degrees warmer and wearing short sleeves. Start a compost pile. Recycle everything you can. Become politically active in the environmental arena. *We all already know all these things and more. The trick is to actually do them.*

4. Pay attention to the seasons and cycles. Our bodies have a rhythm attuned to the natural world. We respond to the hours of daylight and darkness. The Medicine Wheel honors the four cardinal directions and the four seasons. Are you different in the summer at the southern point on the medicine wheel than you are in the winter, when the energy moves north and the days are short? Are you different when the moon passes through each of its four phases? Can you see a correspondence between the seasons and the Holy Days of Judaism, Christianity, and the earth-centered religions? I wrote a book of daily prayers and meditations that honors all religions in accordance with the seasons and cycles. It is called *Pocketful of Miracles*. You might enjoy going through a yearly cycle with it.

5.   Unclutter and beautify your home and workplace. The everyday mystic is attuned to harmony and beauty in the inside world as well as in nature. If your house or office is a mess, and you are truly a Path-One mystic, clutter will drain your energy more than you might imagine. Clean up and remove unnecessary bric-a-brac. *Less is more for the Path-One mystic*. If your space lacks natural light, you will be prone to depression. Get rid of extraneous window coverings and let in both daylight and moonlight to the degree that privacy will allow. Read up on the Chinese art of Feng Shui, or have an expert come and assess your living space. Feng Shui is the art of maximizing the energy flow within structures, a matter of extreme importance to you.

6.   Nurture plants or pets. One of the best ways to tune into the natural world is through gardening. Even if you live in an apartment, you may be able to container-garden on a roof, balcony, or fire escape. And almost every place has a spot where house plants will grow. If you garden mindfully, watching the plants' periods of growth, dormancy, flower, fruiting, and return to Grandmother Earth, you will find that your intuitive abilities will also grow and that you will feel more peaceful and centered. Pets are also important if your living space and lifestyle allow them. I've learned as much about life from dogs, cats, and birds as I have from people. And they have excellent side effects in terms of improving both mood and health, particularly the cardiovascular system.

7. Spend time in the solitude of nature. Charles Eastman wrote, "Speech is to the Indian a perilous gift. He believes profoundly in Silence, the sign of a perfect equilibrium."[4] The first path is indeed one of equilibrium, of balance with nature, of attunement with the Unseen One. Nature meditates us, drawing us into the Web of Life. When I ran a mind/body clinic, we used to have a Sunday program that included a one-hour silent walk—rain or shine. People were told to walk alone, for the experience is totally changed if you talk to another person. The same goes for dogs on a leash who require your attention. This is time for you to be alone in terms of being all-one with nature. Patients reported the most remarkable experiences of unity on their silent mindful walks, proverbial epiphanies like that of seeing the world in a flower. Let nature bring you into God-Union, for this is your path.

※　　※　　※

✳ CHAPTER THREE

Path Two
Creativity and Abundance
Generosity of Spirit

The late Catholic priest Anthony Demello told a wonderful story about a Hindu yogi whose guru left him under a tree on a riverbank to meditate on God. The yogi had only two possessions: his loincloth and a begging bowl. Once a day he walked to the village to beg for food. The rest of the time he spent in contemplation of God. One night he washed out his loincloth and hung it on the tree to dry. When he awakened, it had been chewed up by a rat. With great embarrassment, he begged for both food and a new loincloth that day, and went right back to contemplating God. A few days later he washed out his new loincloth and hung it up to dry. Once again, the rat chewed it up during the night.

What was the yogi to do? It was unseemly for a man of God to keep begging for loincloths. So, he got a kitten to chase the rat. But the kitten was hungry, and soon the yogi had to beg for milk. It was embarrassing to beg for milk, so he found a stray cow. All went well until the summer heat burned off the remaining grasses, and the yogi had to beg fodder for the cow. It wasn't good to have to beg fodder, so when the rainy season came, the yogi planted some crops. They prospered in the rich soil, but so much of his time was spent farming that he could hardly meditate. So he hired laborers to tend his fields, but they needed supervision, which disturbed his meditation. So the yogi decided to take a wife to oversee the workers so that he could get back to God. She didn't want to live under a tree by the river, so they had to build a house—a large house—for she was soon pregnant.

The yogi grew fat and wealthy by the banks of the river. One day when he was sitting under his meditation tree resting, a familiar figure approached. It was his guru, who surveyed the scene with a wide-eyed look, "Student, is that you? Didn't I leave you here five years ago to contemplate God?" The Yogi bowed his head and gestured to his vast estate, "Revered Teacher, I know it seems hard to understand, but truly, this was the only way I could keep my loincloth."

Jesus wrote that one cannot serve both God and mammon; that it is easier for a camel to pass through the eye of a needle than for a rich man to enter the Kingdom of Heaven. And indeed, like the Yogi, it is easy to forget about God-Union when the things of the world are always calling for our attention. Nonetheless, we have to be able to survive physically in the world, use our gifts creatively, and make sufficient money to sustain ourselves. Poverty, as much as wealth for its own sake, can take us away from our search for God.

Jesus said that when we seek the Kingdom of Heaven first, all things shall be added to us. This is a profound spiritual truth, and to fully appreciate it we need to look at the underpinnings of creativity and abundance—our ability to use our active male aspect to stake out a territory in which to use our gifts, and to use our female, receptive aspect as a womb in which to receive the inspiration that grows the gifts. When our male and female aspects combine in a second-chakra sacred marriage, the miracle of creation occurs, and we give birth to fabulous ideas and projects. We manifest spiritual abundance and a generosity of spirit that invites those around us to use their creativity and to share in the abundance that comes when our creative gifts are dedicated to God.

The Flow of Abundance

I once had a scientific colleague we'll call "Nicole," who was psychologically stuck in a perpetual state of lack. She overused her male aspect by staking out her territory rigidly and trying to control everyone in her lab. Her female aspect, however, was undeveloped. She couldn't let herself or others "grow with the flow," receiving inspiration and paying attention to their intuition. No matter how much grant money came in, Nicole believed that the pipeline would dry up and she would be out of a job in research.

She had an active laboratory with many technicians, graduate students, and post-doctoral fellows, all eager to participate in finding a cure for cancer. Competent if uninspired research came out of her group, but there was an undercurrent of discontent. Nicole "nickeled and dimed" her staff to distraction, trying to cut back salaries that were already too low and scrimping on supplies. Every requisition for a pen turned into a nightmare; every long lunch hour became a control issue. The laboratory sputtered along but didn't flourish. A potentially brilliant researcher had dammed up the flow of divine energy, creating scarcity rather than abundance, by trying to control everything and everyone. The creativity that might have manifested in scientific breakthroughs was choked off.

Another colleague by the name of "Richard" had a well-developed female aspect, and trusted that things would move along as they should. He had a continuous flow of bright ideas and designed inspired experiments. Unlike Nicole, however, his male aspect was poorly developed. He didn't control his laboratory and staff enough, providing necessary boundaries, guidance, and discipline. His technician Louise was an alcoholic who often came in hours late, jeopardizing or ruining experiments. Typical of people who have perfected the art of manipulating others, Louise would come up with infinite hard luck stories and Richard would bury his frustration and try to help. Anyone could walk across the borders of Richard's territory and make off with the whole treasury. One by one, the psychologically healthy staff left to work elsewhere and Richard attracted a group of ne'er-do-wells to the perpetual feast of money, time, and energy that he provided. Eventually, he lost his grant funding and the laboratory closed down.

Nicole and Richard are more alike than they are different: two sides of the same coin. Both ran their lives and laboratories out of fear. Nicole feared lack and set boundaries that were too rigid. Richard feared abandonment, so he set no boundaries and got trampled on. Nicole had an undeveloped female aspect, Richard an undeveloped male aspect. The sacred marriage of male and female was, therefore, blocked, and neither could give birth to the divine child of creative science. Although Richard may have appeared generous in giving so much to his staff, his apparent generosity was really a prison in which the ne'er-do-wells foundered, unable to manifest abundance and creativity in their own lives.

Generosity of Spirit

The Path-Two mystic embodies generosity of spirit. True generosity of spirit is a hallmark of good managers, teachers, scientists, therapists, mentors, parents, and friends. The highest intention of those who are generous in spirit is to encourage the creative potential in themselves and others. Because they know they are about God's work, they trust that whatever is needed will be provided. Abundance becomes manifest when one's intention is generous. Doors open unexpectedly, strangers come to our aid, and "surprise money" arrives in time to pay unusual bills or fund important projects.

There is, however, a big difference between faith that the Universe will provide and magical thinking. If you don't have a job or any means of support, it is unlikely that a bundle of money will come tumbling down the chimney, although miracles do happen. You have to do your part as a co-creator to manifest abundance financially, spiritually, creatively, relationally, and in all areas of your life. The Path-Two mystic is a practical person as well as one of faith.

Four things are required to develop generosity of spirit:

1. *The intention to serve God in all our affairs.*

2. *The belief that if that intention is honored, the Universe will provide all that is required materially and spiritually for our success.*

3. *The understanding that we receive as we give, and that our own creativity is enhanced through mentoring others.*

4. *Practical groundedness. God can't deliver the lottery jackpot unless we buy a ticket.[1] We won't have a bestselling book unless we write one.*

What Is True Abundance?

In the sixth chapter of the Gospel of Matthew, Jesus gives a wonderful teaching on abundance:

> Do not lay up for yourselves treasures on earth, where moth and rust consume and where thieves break in and steal, but lay up for yourselves treasures in heaven, where neither moth nor rust consumes and where thieves do not break in and steal. For where your treasure is, there will your heart be also."[2]

The question is, what do you treasure, and what is most important, because that is where you will put your energy, your heart. If you are simply interested in creating wealth and manifesting jaguars, you may be able to do it, but to what end? These are temporary pleasures, and according to some polls, wealth may not be such a pleasure. The very wealthy have a much higher rate of suicide than the rest of us.

We lay up treasures in heaven when we have a strong sense of self-worth that allows us to "grow with the flow," seizing the opportunities that are presented to us. It is a Universal Law that we receive as we give. But remember Richard. Giving people leeway to walk all over you is not generosity; it is fear. It creates lack and exhaustion rather than abundance and energy. Nurse/researcher Dr. Janet Quinn is an expert in Therapeutic Touch (TT). In this simple system of healing, the giver of TT centers herself in God with the intention to be a channel for divine energy. She aligns with the true Self, the best potential in the person she is channeling energy to. Preliminary research of Dr. Quinn found an improvement in immunity not only in the receiver of TT, but also in the giver. This is truly the manifestation of abundance.

In a closed system of energy based on fear and lack, abundance in one place creates lack in another. In an open system of energy, based on faith and love, abundance begets more abundance, and creativity flourishes.

St. Francis of Assisi is a model of spiritual abundance, the true security that comes from knowing that you are a child of God, provided for as you provide for others out of love, rather than fear. His famous prayer has been an inspiration for millions of people:

Lord, make me an instrument of Thy Peace.
Where there is hatred, let me sow love.
Where there is injury, pardon.
Where there is doubt, faith.
Where there is despair, hope.
Where there is darkness, light.
Where there is sadness, joy.

O Divine Master,
grant that I may not so much seek
to be consoled as to console;
to be understood, as to understand;
to be loved, as to love:
for it is in giving that we receive,
it is in pardoning that we are pardoned,
and it is in dying that we are born to Eternal Life.

The Path-Two mystic keeps her eyes on the goal of Eternal Life, knowing that this life is as ephemeral as a dream, and that true abundance lies in our co-creatorship with God.

Suggestions for the Path-Two Mystic

1. Take stock of your boundaries, your territorial male aspect. Are you like Nicole, rigid and withholding, or a doormat like Richard whose boundaries are practically nonexistent? There is no way to pray or meditate your way to better boundaries, although these practices are a general help to psychological growth. Therapy and groups such as Al-Anon or Co-Dependents Anonymous (CODA) are a substantial help for developing healthy boundaries and the self-worth that sustains them.

2. Take stock of your ability to "grow with the flow," the creative, receptive female aspect. Are you open to new ideas, to the power of dreams, intuition, and synchronicities? Are you willing to follow hunches and throw out ideas and projects in which you have already invested time, money, and effort if your gut tells you to move elsewhere? Can you give yourself permission to brainstorm, which means permission to be wrong, in order to keep the creative energy flowing?

3. Do your part to manifest abundance practically. God helps those who help themselves. If you are not manifesting creativity and abundance in your work, relationships, and finances, take a look at the practical side of things. It is one thing to plant seeds, another to follow through with the watering and weeding. God creates the miracle of growth through which the seed manifests its full potential as a flower, but we need to cooperate in the gardening. Do you need to train for a different job? Are you practicing generosity of spirit in the workplace? Is your workplace dysfunctional? If so, do you need to move on, or can you help facilitate positive change?

4. In God We Trust. Have you looked at a piece of money lately? These are the words that our forefathers engraved on our currency. There is an important message here for manifesting abundance financially and in all areas of our life. An Hasidic teaching states that when we take one step toward God, He takes a hundred steps toward us. Try thanking God in advance for the abundance and creativity in your life, trusting that you will receive it:

> *"Thank you, God, for this healthy body that enjoys Your Creation and is Your eyes and ears, head and heart, hands and feet upon this earth. Thank you God for my loving family and friends and the beautiful ways that we help bring one another fully into being. Thank you, God, for allowing me to fulfill my intention of bringing Your Love to others. Thank you, God, for the meaningful work You have given me to do, and for the ears to hear what I need to do today. Thank you, God, for the material abundance in my life, the food that nourishes my body, the love that nourishes my soul, the money that allows me to sustain myself and enjoy all the benefits of [add your particular blessings]."*

5. What is your creative intention? If your intention in manifesting abundance is limited to storing up treasures on earth, the moths and rust will eventually get the better of you. What is the one creative intention that summarizes your spiritual treasure, the creative gifts you can give? Like St. Francis, it may be to be an instrument of God's peace. For me, it is to be an instrument of God's love and healing. For you it may be to be an instrument of God's ability to manufacture safe cars, to provide excellent customer service, to raise psychologically, emotionally, and spiritually healthy children, to cure cancer, or to create community. Write out your intention clearly and repeat it to yourself and God each morning, giving thanks for the opportunity to use your gifts in service of all.

6. Count your blessings. Is the glass half empty or half full? The poorest welfare recipients in the United States are wealthy beyond belief in the eyes of most of the rest of the world. Even street people have resources available to them that those in developing countries can only dream about. When is the last time you were thankful for your toilet or toaster? For having a change of clothes or a pair of shoes? For the idea to call a friend that led to some interesting joint venture? My computer is definitely a Godsend. It is easy to fall into yearning for what we lack rather than gratitude for what we have. Give thanks for what you have, and abundance will fill your life.

7. Give to charity. Find at least one cause that you can put your heart and soul into. Whether it is prison reform, feeding the hungry, saving the environment, or any other cause that moves you, commit to supporting it. In observant Jewish households, it is customary to place money in the "pushke," the charity box in your home, every Friday night before the Sabbath begins. Make a charity box for your home, and once a week call your family together to contribute to it. Decide how much money each of you can give and at what intervals you will send it in. Collecting actual currency from every family member is much more energizing than the designated bill payer writing a check that is relatively impersonal.

❈   ❈   ❈

✳️ CHAPTER FOUR

Path Three
How Can I Help?
The Passion To Serve

The Reverend Dr. Martin Luther King was a man of God, a man with a mission to open human hearts to the equality of all people, regardless of race. One of the most passionate orators of all time, his 1963 "I Have a Dream" speech was so filled with powerful emotion that it galvanized an entire generation to work for civil rights. Do you remember his words?: *"I have a dream that one day this nation will rise up and live out the true meaning of its creed....We hold these truths to be self-evident: that all men are created equal."*

Speaking to people of color who were ready to erupt into violence, he met the power of angry discontent with the fiery passion of God's love: *"Let us not seek to satisfy our thirst for freedom by drinking from the cup of bitterness and hatred....Again and again we must rise to the majestic heights of meeting physical force with soul force."*

When ideas are fortified with passionate emotion, they become powerful thought-forms etched in the mass mind like technicolor icons on God's great computer. It is then easy for other people to tune into these enduring symbols. All we have to do to think of nonviolence and human rights is to conjure up the memory of Martin Luther King. He may have been assassinated physically in 1968, but King's message is eternal and indestructible. The assassination, in fact, made King a martyr, the archetype of the Path-Three mystic who is willing to give all he has to fulfill his dream, God's dream.

Whom Do I Serve?

The defining question for the Path-Three mystic is: Whom do I serve—myself or God? King was interested in serving God through freeing his people, as was another great mystic and social activist, Mahatma Gandhi. Both embraced the tactics of nonviolence, for while the third-chakra, fire-in-the-belly, faces-the-East mystic wields enormous power, it is the power of peace and understanding. We have all witnessed powerful orators, whether politicians or salespeople, who can capture our attention. But all too often, their primary interest is in serving themselves by garnering fame, fortune, power, or prestige.

When the powerful energy of the solar plexus, the inner sun, is used selfishly, it can lead to corruption, violence, and the enslavement of others. Think about the dictators of countries who serve the interests of the rich by exploiting the poor, or people such as Saddam Hussein, whose lust for power unleashed senseless war in the Middle East. Adolf Hitler is one of the most sinister examples of Path-Three power gone wrong. He was a brilliant orator with an uncanny ability to feed off and increase the energy of a crowd. But his dream of creating a perfect race was evil. Rather than celebrating the perfection of diversity, he sought to create a "Master Race" of Aryans by destroying Jews, gypsies, and other "foreigners," as well as anyone who dared to disagree with him. Intense charisma like Hitler's is often a quality of those who have the potential to use their passion to manifest a dream. But without the desire to serve God, charismatic people can easily be subverted in the service of evil.

The Source of Power

When asked about his healing power, Jesus replied that he of himself did nothing; rather, it was the Father who worked through him. I once asked a Sufi (Islamic mystic) healer a similar question about the source of healing power. He replied that there were two sources for a healer to tap into. The first was a personal source—the healer's own adrenal glands. And the adrenals are indeed the furnace that generates lifeforce energy.

We are all familiar with the fight-or-flight response that enables a 110-pound mother to generate the superhuman energy to lift a truck off her injured child. The passionate emotional response to her suffering little one triggers the release of adrenalin from the medulla, or central core, of the adrenal glands. The adrenalin increases heart rate and blood pressure, shifts the brain into super-quick thinking, and causes a massive release of stored sugar to fuel the muscles. Adrenalin gives us the power to work to meet deadlines, to run marathons, and to get the house cleaned in record time before company comes! Nonetheless, we pay a price for constantly calling on adrenal energy. It is called burnout. When that happens, we've depleted the adrenals so severely that our energy for even commonplace tasks is low.

The second source of healing power comes from God. Rather than generating and using personal energy, we become channels for divine energy. This source of power is limitless. Like the sun that rises in the east, it is renewed each day. It can't run out, and we can't burn out. *The most important factor in becoming a channel for divine energy—whether we use it for healing or to manifest our dreams—is humility.* Webster's dictionary defines humility as "the absence of pride." Pride, in turn, is defined as an "overhigh opinion of oneself," or conceit. The old adage, "Pride goeth before a fall," refers to the loss of power that accompanies conceit. Personal power is always limited. Sooner or later we will hit the wall. But truly humble people, such as Jesus and all the great healers and mystics, know that they are a *channel* for power—and not its source. This very attitude of humility is what allow's God's power to flow through them.

Your Life Purpose

I believe that many of us will never truly know our life purpose while in human form. The old Hasidic rabbis said that even many of the great *tzaddiks,* or saints, didn't know their life purpose because that knowledge was likely to create conceit. Perhaps your purpose in life is actually a chance remark that you make to a friend in an elevator: "My husband used to drive me nuts with his jealousy, but we've both learned a lot about it in therapy. You know, I think relationships are places where old childhood wounds come up so that we can heal each other."

The man standing next to you, who was on his way to the lawyer's office to file for divorce, suddenly has the goosebumpy feeling of *deus ex machina*, like God is floating in from the wings in a play. Your remark pierces his heart, and he has a revelation about relationships. Instead of going to the lawyer, he decides that he is ready to give therapy a try, a suggestion that his wife has made repeatedly. The results are so heartening that the man quits his job, retrains as a therapist, and writes a bestselling book that helps thousands of people to heal in relationship—all because of your chance remark.

We are all interconnected and help bring one another into the expression of our full potential through words, thoughts, and deeds that are unimaginable in their simplicity and untraceable in their complexity. The man that you inspired in the elevator found his passion in life. It may or may not be his primary life purpose, but for the sake of operational definitions, when I talk about life purpose I really mean our passion—what comes naturally and what feeds the fire in our belly.

Do you remember the last time you felt truly passionate about an idea or a person? Passionate attraction leads to a wild, wonderful state in which energy abounds. Need to drive 100 miles to tryst with your lover after work, then drive home and go to work again the next morning? No problem in the heightened state that infatuation creates. All things seem possible; all obstacles exciting challenges to surmount. In the case of infatuation with a lover, the spell and the energizing biochemical changes that it weaves, wear off in a few months. In the case of a dream to which we are committed, such as helping others heal from their wounds, the spell may last for a lifetime. And for as long as we are passionate about our dream, we will have the energy to bring it into manifestation. Perhaps this is what the late mythologist Joseph Campbell was thinking about when he said, "Follow your bliss."

Are You A Path-Three Mystic?

Many people are dedicated to service without necessarily being Path-Three mystics. In fact, all the spiritual paths embody service, but for a Path-Three mystic, the need to serve is a consuming passion. For example, I follow my bliss, love my work as a writer and teacher, and am deeply committed to serving God by helping people heal spiritually, emotionally, and physically. But I am definitely not a Path-Three mystic. I am too fond of leisure time, long walks, lazy reveries, hanging out with family and friends, puttering in the garden, playing with the dogs and the cat, and avidly reading mystery novels to work ceaselessly on behalf of a dream.

The true fire-in-the-belly mystic has such passion that it occupies not only his daytime work, but his nighttime dreams. He lives and breathes this passion as a form of dedication to God and humanity. His charisma and effectiveness stem from humility, and he leaves a lasting impression on those that he touches. All Path-Three mystics, however, are not famous. Some of those who work for organizations such as Greenpeace, placing themselves between huge factory ships and hunted whales, have the passion required to give their lives for their beliefs. People who challenge giant conglomerates that pollute the air and water may also be Path-Three mystics, rallying others to the cause and challenging giants like Goliath with a slingshot made powerful by their dedication to God.

Suggestions for the Path-Three Mystic

1. Beware of Power. It has been said that power has the ability to corrupt. It is easy to lose one's humility and fall into the belief that you, rather than God, are the source of the important work you are doing. When this happens, the power flowing through you slows down, and it becomes tempting to use your own power, which is far less effective and may even compromise your integrity. Some of the psychic healers that practice in the Phillippines have been discussed in this regard. The original healers worked from a wholehearted dedication to God, using the unusual gift of being able to reach through a person's energy body and pull out diseased tissue as an energy form, which then manifested as actual physical tissue. When people began to flock to them for healing, some of the healers became prideful and lost their gift. When the healing charism—the paranormal gift—departed, some of these people became charlatans, using sleight of hand and chicken tissue to mimic the diseased human tissue they were supposedly removing.

2. Beware of charisma. People are naturally attracted to charismatic, or gifted, individuals. If you take this attraction personally—forgetting that the real attraction is to God shining through you—you may end up in unwanted personal entanglements. The attraction that people feel for you may also take a sexual form. Witness the large number of preachers, spiritual teachers, and politicians who compromise themselves sexually, hurt people deeply, and end up losing their positions or their credibility.

3.   Seek conscious communion with God. If your intention is to serve God, a meditation practice that opens you to divine guidance is important. Father Thomas Keating, a Trappist monk, is abbot of the Snowmass monastery in Colorado and a consummate teacher of centering prayer—a movement into interior silence in which your focus is on being present to God. One adopts a prayer word (my own is *shalom,* meaning "peace" and "welcome") to use when the mind becomes busy and distracted from the intention of opening to God's presence. Anything other than the velvety silence of interior quiet is a distraction, including wonderful insights, visitations from the saints, or any thoughts whatsoever. The fruits of centering prayer are less likely to be in the practice session than at other times during the day when you are going about your business and are suddenly aware of God's presence, because you have diligently cultivated your openness. Complete instructions can be found in Keating's valuable book, *Open Mind, Open Heart.*

4.   Take time for yourself. A person with passion and charisma is generally busy and in demand. Doing God's work is wonderful, but you will last longer if you take time out to rest and care for yourself physically and emotionally. Healthful food, time in nature, and the pursuit of a hobby or handicraft can help keep you in top form. Some of the best creative ideas come in leisure moments when our own mind quiets, and God can get a word in edgewise. The history of creativity is full of such examples. The great mathematician Poincaré had a breakthrough on a problem he had been puzzling over while stepping off a bus while touring the French countryside.

5. Nurture your relationships. Spend time with family and friends. Relationships are sacred, for in them we come to know ourselves more deeply, to heal and be healed. And relationships require time and attention. Even the people you love will grow resentful if you take that love for granted. Plan times to go away with family or friends and make that time inviolate—no work. Becoming isolated and out of touch is a hazard for the Path-Three mystic—not only because relationships are so important personally—but also because our friends and loved ones are best able to give us feedback about where we may be going off-track.

6. Cultivate a sense of humor. The third chakra is the site of belly laughter. One of the occupational hazards of living your passion is becoming so serious that you block the flow of energy. Taking yourself too seriously is a sign of growing pride and conceit. Besides which, who wants to live with an uptight workaholic? No matter how wonderful your contribution may be, you are still just one more Bozo on the bus. Humorist Loretta LaRoche reminds us that life is a joke, and that we are it. She does a wonderful routine in which she mimics how uptight we get, with pursed lips and squeezed-up behinds that can hold a quarter between the cheeks. Loosen up, laugh a little, and drop that quarter.

7. Cultivate patience. Even Rome was not built in a day. Inventors often work for years, discarding ideas that don't work before they finally bring their dream into being. What most people consider patience is actually impatience stretched to the limit. Even dreams and ideas that are fully formed may take a long time to get into circulation. Have faith. If you serve God, your very act of service is the most important outcome. The results of that service are up to God, not you. Perhaps the hardest lesson to learn is not to be attached to the results of our actions.

❄   ❄   ❄

Chapter Five

Path Four
The Way of the Heart
Bridging Earth and Heaven

Once upon a time there was a failing monastery. No new postulants had entered for years, and the remaining monks were a crabby lot, always complaining about one another. The abbot was concerned that the monastery would close, so he prayed to God for guidance. One day he got the idea to visit his old friend the rabbi, and poured out his feelings about the troubled monastery and despondent monks. The two then sat companionably, sipping tea, while the rabbi regarded his friend with a puzzled look.

"But don't you realize that one of you is the Messiah?"

The abbot's eyes grew round. "What, one of us, the Messiah? We are plain and simple men. How could that possibly be?"

"Trust me, dear friend. God works in mysterious ways," smiled the rabbi.

All the way back to the monastery, the abbot turned over the thought in his mind. One of them, the Messiah? Who on earth could it possibly be? Surely not Brother Paul, the slovenly cook. But why not? Doesn't God delight in nourishing his children? Absolutely not Brother Raymond, that silly joker, always acting the fool. But didn't Jesus say that we must become again like little children to enter the Kingdom of Heaven? What about Brother Michael the gardener, so silent and taciturn? But maybe he isn't taciturn after all, just caught up in an inner communion. Doesn't he commune with the flowers and animals like St. Francis, the very patron saint of their order?

The abbot called all the monks together and announced that he had shocking news. One of them was the Messiah. The news jolted everyone and they began to regard each other with new respect. Every word and action was interpreted as a gift from God. An abundance of love poured from the monks, through their hearts and eyes, and nourished everything they looked upon. The gardens grew more beautiful and the food more delicious. People began to show up again for Sunday Mass. And soon, young men began to apply for admission to the order. [1]

To See God in Each Other

A reporter once asked Mother Teresa what the purpose of human life was. She responded like a true Path-Four mystic: "To give and receive love." In the beautiful collection of her teachings, *No Greater Love*, she says, "What is my spiritual life? A love union with Jesus in which the divine and the human give themselves completely to one another."[2] She expresses this union in two major ways that are like sides of the same coin: service to others and devotion to Jesus. When she picks up a dying person from the streets of Calcutta, Mother Teresa sees them as Jesus—as the Messiah in her Christian devotional path. Whatever she does for others, she does for God. But to see the Messiah in others, we must first recognize him within ourselves.

In 1893, Swami Vivekananda arrived in Chicago to speak at the first World Parliament of Religions. He was the first Hindu ever to address the American public, and his lectures were shocking to fundamentalists who regarded his teachings of humankind's inner divinity as heinous blasphemy. Vivekananda often told the story of a lion who had been raised by a flock of sheep and naturally thought that he was one of them. Another lion tried to convince him that he was not a sheep after all, but to no avail until he took the "sheep-lion" to a pool and showed him his true reflection. *"And you are lions," Vivekananda would tell the audience, "you are pure, infinite and perfect souls.... He, for whom you have been weeping and praying in churches and temples, is your own Self."[3]*

For the Hindu, God dwells within each person as their essential *Self*, what the Buddhists call the *rigpa*, or our own true nature. *Finding God is therefore an inner search rather than an outer one.* The Self or rigpa is like a sun that shines within our heart, but is hidden by clouds of doubt, fear, guilt, and confusion. The clouds are sustained by the ego, or false self, which imagines itself unworthy and separate from other people and God. The path to God is in dismantling the ego, parting the clouds so that the true Self, the inner divinity, can shine through and we can recognize that the Messiah has always been within us.

The Eastern notion that God is found within is mirrored by many Western holy men. The German Catholic mystic, Meister Eckhart, wrote that "God is not found in the soul by adding anything but by a process of subtraction."[4] This, indeed, is the point of meditation. By subtracting the chatter in our minds that is constantly recreating the world of the sheep, we approach the clear inner pool in which our true reflection as a lion is revealed. In addition to finding our Self spiritually, however, we must also find it psychologically.

When I ran a mind/body clinic at Harvard, the principal problem that most people shared was self-criticism and low self-esteem. Most felt that if you really knew them, you wouldn't like them. Students, housewives, physicians, and bank presidents all shared this basic wound, regardless of their worldly success. Most people felt guilty not just about things they had done, but about who they were. They just didn't feel as though they were good enough. This shame and guilt carried over into their relationship with God, a fact that was underscored by the results of a questionnaire that revealed that the majority of patients actually believed that their illness was a punishment for their sins. I wrote the book *Guilt Is the Teacher, Love Is the Lesson* as a primer on healing the wound of unworthiness and coming closer to God.

Being Yourself

There is an old Hasidic story about Rabbi Zuszya, who dies and goes to heaven. While reviewing his life, he explains to God that he had tried to be as wise as Solomon, as steadfast as David, and as brave as Moses. "That is all well and good," replies God, "but why didn't you try to be yourself?"

Each person is unique and important to the Whole we call God. If every part of the body tried to be the brain, the eyes, or the heart, there would be no body. The lungs and liver, the gallbladder, the intestines, the hands, feet, and fingers—every part is necessary and precious to the Whole. In our society, we put inordinate emphasis on prestige possessions and high-paying jobs. Many children grow up with the idea that the best job is to be president. In the social circle in which I was raised, medicine and law were considered the best careers. I still remember how shocked my parents were when the son of our family doctor dropped out of Harvard Medical School to pursue his love of the arts. While his parents only wanted "the best" for him, he was supposed to conform to their image rather than his own. It takes courage to find and express our true gifts, especially if they are not recognized by others.

I once met a young man who was a cashier in an airport gift shop. He looked at me with as much respect and love as if I were, indeed, the Messiah. And he helped me with such care and courtesy that I felt uplifted for days. His smile touched my heart, and I feel sure that when he stands before God he will be praised for having been truly himself, and for loving others as himself. This young man had a job that few people would aspire to. He was not a doctor or a lawyer. He wasn't Moses, Solomon, or David. But he was one of the most important people I have ever met. He was truly himself, and in that act, he was a servant of God who inspired and uplifted others. In his gentle graciousness and humility, this uncelebrated Path-Four mystic united earth and heaven in his heart.

Some people are born into fortunate circumstances in which their parents know what it is to love and nurture children. They are encouraged, challenged, and guided into becoming the unique expression of God that they are. But most of us were born to parents who were still learning to love themselves and passed on their doubts, fears, and wounds to us, as well as their love. While the majority of parents did the best they could, we may still have work to do as adults, turning the wounds of childhood into wisdom and compassion. One of the most important ways in which we learn to do this is through the practice of forgiveness.

To Err Is Human, To Forgive Divine

Forgiveness is one of the least understood of all spiritual practices. It has nothing to do with condoning poor behavior in ourselves and others. Rather, it calls us to responsibility. *In forgiving ourselves, we make the journey from guilt for what we have done (or not done) to celebration of what we have become.* This transformation of heart comes about through reflecting on the results of our mistakes, understanding how ignorance or woundedness created those actions, and doing the necessary healing so that we will do better next time. Error calls us to repentance, which means literally to think again. It is the crucible in which the soul is forged and the psyche healed. Mistakes, in fact, are sacred because of the powerful potential for growth that they contain.

A *Time* magazine article on forgiveness called it a shrewd strategy for a nation or a person to follow because forgiveness sets the forgiver free. Whether we hold on to blaming ourselves or someone else, unforgiveness is like an anchor that keeps us from moving on. It is the jailer of the soul. You probably know people who are still blaming someone who has been dead for years. What does the resentment serve? Its only effect is to create stress and prevent the flow of lifeforce energy—leading to fatigue, disease, and depression. The Buddha compared resentment to a hot coal that we pick up with the intent of throwing it at someone else, only to be burned ourselves. To forgive is to put down the coal.

Time and time again, Jesus taught that we are forgiven as we forgive others, that what we bind on earth is bound in heaven, and that what we let loose on earth is let loose in heaven. Why bind our hearts? Isn't it preferable to let loose compassion? The process of forgiving the people who have wronged us is often long and arduous, particularly if the crime was terrible: child abuse, rape, or murder. Yet some of the wisest and most compassionate people I know are those who took the journey of the heart and forgave the father who molested them or the drunk driver who killed their child.

Jesus may have been able to turn the other cheek, but most of us need to go through a process of venting our anger and feeling grief over our injuries before we can develop compassion for the woundedness in another person that led to their bad deeds. To "forgive" prematurely, before we have harvested the wisdom of our wounds, is like spraying cologne on garbage. Soon the stench will rise again. We have to be gentle with ourselves when forgiveness takes time to accomplish. And we have to understand that forgiveness is freedom of mind and heart, not an invitation to be hurt again. Once we have forgiven our enemies, we are under no obligation to invite them for dinner, let them out of jail, or speak to them again unless appropriate.

The Path of Devotion

Many religious traditions help us find forgiveness and respect for ourselves and others through the study and imitation of spiritual mentors such as Moses, Jesus, Mary, Krishna, or the saints. Sometimes when I get into an emotional bind, I wonder to myself how Mary Magdalene—one of my heroines—might have responded. In that process, I actually begin to merge with her. The Hindus call the practice of God-Union through merging or devotion *bhakti* yoga. But you can find elements of devotion in all religions. Some Jews are devoted to the Torah, the first five books of the Old Testament that Moses received on Mt. Sinai, worshiping the Torah as if she were a woman, spending almost every waking hour trying to merge with her wisdom. Catholics imagine God in three persons: the Father, the Son, and the Holy Spirit; and many also worship the aspect of God as Mother through devotion to Mary.

In Mexico, for example, shrines to the Virgin of Guadalupe are abundant, and her intercession is sought daily by millions who love her as a personal reflection of a more abstract God. Hindus similarly imagine God in different persons such as Brahma, Krishna, and Shiva; as well as Kali the Mother. Buddhists, too, may be devoted to various gods, goddesses, and wisdom figures who become the center of their daily prayers and practices. By devotion to a guru or teacher who has already merged with some aspect of God, many Hindus and Buddhists also hope to achieve God-Union.

Ramakrishna, for example, was a celebrated Hindu holy man of the 1800s. He had an intense devotion to the Divine Mother, and, for years, dressed in women's clothing and sat around with the women of his village, trying to merge himself with the feminine principle. While such behavior would be ridiculed in Western culture, it was perfectly acceptable in India, where even today every truck and taxi has a flower-laden shrine to the family god on the dashboard, and stores have names like Gurukripa (guru's grace) pastry or tailor shop.

In Native American vision quests, the seeker devotes himself to the service of his tribe, opening himself to merge with the spirit of an animal who will bring wisdom for the group and henceforth be his personal guide. Carrying totems of the power animal, and seeking guidance from this aspect of the Great Mystery, is also a kind of devotion. And the fruits of devotion in all paths are the same: love, respect, kindness, service, and a peaceful heart.

Suggestions for the Path-Four Mystic

1. Try the practice of metta, or lovingkindness meditation, as it is called in the Buddhist tradition. In this meditation, you will send blessings first to yourself, then to your loved ones, then to those you are in conflict with, and finally to all beings. The Buddhists obviously knew that unless we filled the chalice of our own heart first, there would be nothing there to give to others:

Close your eyes and begin by taking a few letting-go breaths, and then enter the inner sanctuary of stillness...Imagine a great star of light above you, pouring a waterfall of love and light over you....Let the light enter the top of your head and wash through you, revealing the purity of your own heart, which expands and extends beyond you, merging with the Divine Light....See yourself totally enclosed in the egg of light, and then repeat these lovingkindness blessings for yourself:

May I be at peace, May my heart remain open,
May I awaken to the light of my own true nature,
May I be healed, May I be a source of healing
for all beings.

Next, bring loved ones to mind. See them in as much detail as possible, imagining the loving light shining down on them and washing through them, revealing the light within their own heart. Imagine this light growing brighter, merging with the Divine light and enclosing them in the egg of light. Then bless them:

May you be at peace, May your heart remain open,
May you awaken to the light of your own true nature,

*May you be healed, May you be a source
of healing for all beings.*

Repeat this for as many people as you wish.

Next, think of a person whom you hold in judgment, and to whom you're ready to begin extending forgiveness. Place him or her in the egg of light, and see the light washing away all negativity and illusion, just as it did for you and your loved ones. Bless this person:

*May you be at peace, May your heart remain open,
May you awaken to the light of your own true nature,
May you be healed, May you be a source
of healing for all beings.*

See our beautiful planet as it appears from outer space, a delicate jewel spinning slowly in the starry vastness.... Imagine the earth surrounded by light-green continents, the blue waters, the white polar caps....The two-leggeds and four-leggeds, the fish that swim and the birds that fly....Earth is a place of opposites....Day and night, good and evil, up and down, male and female. Be spacious enough to hold it all as you offer these blessings:

*May there be peace on earth,
May the hearts of all people
be open to themselves and to each other,*

May all people awaken to the light of their
own true nature,
May all creation be blessed and be
a blessing to All That Is.

2. Practice self-forgiveness. Before sleep, review your day, beginning with evening and working back toward morning. Did you do, think, or say anything for which you feel regret? If so, think about what contributed to the situation(s) and whether anything needs to be put right. Do you need to make amends to someone or make some change in your life? Commit to taking any necessary actions, and give thanks for what you have learned. Then ask God to forgive you, as you have forgiven yourself.

3. Forgive others. As you are reviewing your day, notice whether you are resentful of anyone else. Think about what they said or did. Reflect on whether their action was most likely intentional or not. If there is some response you need to make, resolve to do it, and then begin the process of mentally letting go. Imagine the person in your mind's eye. Either pray for their highest good, meaning a heartfelt hope that their full potential will be reached, or send them a lovingkindness blessing. Then enclose them in a bubble of light, and send them into the divine light. You did your part, now let God do the rest.

4. See God in other people. The Sanskrit word *Namaste* is often repeated with a little bow, hands in the prayer pose, as a greeting. This is a salute to the God within the other person, and a recognition of the God within yourself. Implicit in the greeting is the idea that when you are in your God-Self, and the other person is in theirs, you are one. Without repeating "Namaste" out loud, think this word (or something similar from your own tradition) whenever you meet someone. For example, I often say a silent "Shalom" or "Peace be with you" as I try to convey deep respect through my smile, words, and actions.

5. Practice devotion. What aspect of God are you most attracted to? Jesus, Mary, Buddha, Kwan Yin (the Chinese female goddess of compassion), the Torah? God as Grandmother Earth or Grandfather Sky? A classical devotional practice is one in which you actually merge yourself with some aspect of God. Saying the rosary, for example, is a devotion to Mary and a way of becoming one with her. Hindus and Buddhists also use rosaries of 108 beads, called *malas,* on which they repeat a mantra meant to bring them into divine union. The classic Sanskrit mantra *Om Namah Shivaya*, for example, means salutations to Shiva, with the understanding that Shiva is also your inner Self. The Jewish practice of kissing the *mezuzah,* which hangs on the doorpost, is meant as a spur to devotion. The mezuzah contains a scroll upon which the holiest prayer of Judaism is written. It is a reminder to love God with all your heart, soul, and mind and to think of God as you rise up and lie down, as you come in and go out, as you walk upon your way, and as you teach this to your children.

6.   Maintain an active prayer life. In his marvelous book, *Healing Words: The Power of Prayer and the Practice of Medicine*, physician Larry Dossey reviews the entire scientific literature on prayer. Without a doubt, your prayers help people to recover physically and emotionally, even if they don't believe in it. But it won't do to be a cosmic busybody. What if you pray for the physical recovery of a sick friend, and their soul would be better served by a more prolonged struggle with the illness that prompts a deeper search for God and Self? Stick to what Dossey calls *nondirected prayer*, a simple prayer for the person's highest good, whatever that may be. Let yourself off the hook as the Great Divine Director of the Universe who knows what's best. That job's already taken.

7.   Let music open your heart to God. At the women's spiritual retreats that I direct many weekends each year, people come from different religious traditions. Many women are alienated from their religion of origin, and some are even angry at God or the clergy. Yet, when they hear the spiritual music from their childhood, the door of their hearts often fly open. After years of being estranged from Judaism, I went to a Sabbath service, and the songs and dancing seemed to resonate in the very DNA of my cells. I recalled the songs of childhood and the sweet, innocent communion with God that accompanied them. I now begin each day with a Jewish chant called *Modeh Ani*, which is a song of thanksgiving that God, with infinite compassion, has returned my soul to my body again this morning. I have often taught patients to meditate using a sung chant that then moves to a mental chant.

When I asked one elderly Greek Orthodox man where he felt the most peace, he told me it was in church when they sang the *Kyrie Eleison*, a Greek chant that means "Lord Jesus Christ have mercy on me." We sang it together for several minutes, and then he used it as the focus of a silent meditation. When we were finished meditating, he commented that he had a profound sense of connection with all the people, across eons of time, who had ever chanted that prayer.

※　　※　　※

CHAPTER SIX

Path Five
Discipline, Ethics, and Will
Thy Will, Not Mine, Be Done

Two monks were walking at sunrise by the banks of a stream, swollen by the early spring rains. As they rounded a bend, they spied a young woman standing in the middle of the stream, holding up her heavy skirt, which was dripping with icy water. She had lost her footing while trying to scramble from rock to rock, and frightened tears slid down her beautiful face. The older monk hitched up his robe, strode out into the stream, and scooped up the woman in his arms. Having carried her safely across, he deposited her gently on the other bank. She thanked him with great relief, and the two monks resumed their journey.

When the sun set, and the monks were released from the vow of silence they kept during daylight hours, the younger monk turned to his brother with fury, shaking his fists and shouting, "How could you have picked up that woman! You know we have vowed never even to look at a woman, let alone touch one. You have broken your vows, sullied your honor, and offended God."

The older monk smiled patiently at the younger man and replied, "My dearest brother, I put that woman down on the other bank of the stream ten hours ago. You are the one who has been carrying her around all day."

Moral Dilemmas

While the younger monk was true to the letter of the law, keeping the discipline of his vows, the older monk responded to a higher morality—the distress of another human being. St. Paul might have referred to such an act as being beyond the law, but transcending the law in order to serve a higher morality is only an option for those who are truly responding to the will of God. And it is easy to delude oneself on this point. When, if ever, is war a moral act for a person who truly honors the commandment, "Thou shalt not kill"? Peace Pilgrim, a remarkable woman who criss-crossed the United States on foot 17 times, carrying nothing more than a toothbrush and a comb and speaking to large audiences about peace, spoke eloquently on this point. The old saying that there are no atheists in foxholes prompted her to say that there should be no Christians in foxholes either. We might add to that no Jews, Buddhists, Moslems, or any other person whose religious precepts forbid killing. And yet, the history of the world has been bloodied not only by secular wars, but by Holy Wars in which people kill one another in the very name of God.

The Path-Five mystic thinks seriously about such oxymorons as Holy War. When does a higher morality overturn one of the Ten Commandments, the Tibetan precepts for right living, or the Hindu precepts of raja yoga? When, if ever, is war justified, or killing another person? In the Hindu religious classic, the *Bhagavad-Gita* or *The Song of God*, the main character Arjuna finds himself embroiled in a civil war where brother fights brother, student fights teacher. Arjuna throws down his weapons in anguish over the evil of killing. His charioteer is none other than the god Krishna, and a lengthy discussion about good, evil, and war takes place. Krishna argues that the body may be killed, but the spirit is immortal. Life is like a play in which we all constantly take different parts, and the most important thing is for Arjuna to do his duty as a warrior, with his heart fixed upon God, with no attachment to the results of his actions. Arjuna is still despondent and confused, reluctant to kill.

The greatest evil, opines Krishna, is to shirk the duty God has given you, to weasel out of your life purpose. Arjuna must think: What is my duty? What purpose has God given me? The summary of the message is that Arjuna is a warrior who must take his part in the drama, submitting his will to God's will, and act without letting his own desires get in the way of his duty. The dialogue continues, and the nature of God, the mind, reincarnation, and morality are discussed. At the end of the discussion, Arjuna picks up his weapons and goes to war.

Were you Arjuna, would you have been convinced? This is a serious issue for aspiring Path-Five mystics who may, in fact, believe that acts of murder and mayhem are their divinely ordained life purpose. If you believe that abortion violates the commandment not to kill, for example, is it your right to stop others from choosing abortion? Most of us would agree that waging war in the name of God by bombing abortion clinics or shooting the personnel are seriously misguided acts. They fly in the face of the most important commandment, which is to love God and love your neighbor as yourself.

Fanaticism and the submersion of love by fear, dog the history of religion. The rigidity of the medieval Catholic Church, for example, gave rise to the Crusades, during which infidels such as Moslems and Jews were slain to advance the message of Christianity. Contemporary Moslem fundamentalists likewise believe that their *jihads*, or Holy Wars, are divinely ordained. Furthermore, to be killed in a jihad is a one-way ticket to heaven. The passionate, single-minded, and disciplined individuals drawn to the fifth path walk a fine line in distinguishing human from divine will. When an aspiring Path-Five mystic enters the orbit of a charismatic, powerful religious leader who has become unbalanced—like David Koresh, Jim Jones, or some of the Ayatollahs—they may find that they have surrendered to a confused human will rather than to God's Will.

Following Path Five is a difficult journey, both because of the discipline and the level of psychological development that are required. If a person has unhealed wounds from childhood, for example, and needs the support and approval of others to feel good about herself, she may be likely to join a group where adherence to the rules guarantees love and acceptance. She turns her will and judgment over to the group to feel safe. Only a person secure in herself, with the capacity to avoid the black-and-white thinking that accompanies low self-esteem, can walk the fifth path in comfort and safety. Otherwise, the rules of right living can end up as weapons turned on self or others.

Discipline and Justice

The story of the Ten Commandments will give you a flavor for the fifth path. After the exodus from slavery in Egypt, Moses ascended Mt. Sinai to meet God face to face. The Israelites stood below, trembling at the spectacle: the sound of the trumpet, violent thunder and lightning, and the mountain smoking. Moses came down from Sinai, not only with the Ten Commandments, but also with a code of justice.[1] Parts of the code are now thankfully archaic. For example, it outlined laws for buying and selling slaves, including rules for fathers selling their daughters into slavery. It also meted out an eye-for-an-eye type of justice. Whoever killed would be killed. Whoever struck a parent would be also be put to death, as would any woman considered a sorceress.

Some of the laws, however, still make sense today. If you get into a fight and injure your opponent, you have to pay for their lost time and medical bills. If your neighbor's ox falls into an uncovered pit on your property, you have to make good. For every breach of trust, you are instructed to pay double to the injured party. If you lend money to the poor, no interest can be collected. The land can be tilled for only six years, and in the seventh it must lie fallow. Absolute kindness to strangers, widows, and children is expected of everyone. This is the bottom line for the true Path-Five mystic. Without compassion and kindness, justice can turn to cruelty and mockery of the loving presence of God.

All religions have codes of ethics such as the Ten Commandments. These codes serve two functions. First, they keep community life flowing smoothly by prohibiting disruptive acts such as murder, theft, adultery, slander, and covetousness; and by promoting positive behaviors such as charity, honoring one's elders, and worshiping God. Second, they help the individual to develop willpower. Will, after all, is the primal energy of creation. It motivates all behaviors, and without it, life degenerates to chaos. Without the most basic form of will, the will to live, an individual disconnects from the flow of divine energy and simply dies. When will is strongly focused through discipline and ethics, the individual learns how to use energy co-creatively with God.

While most people would agree that honoring the Ten Commandments, the Buddhist Precepts for living, or other codes of ethics is a good idea, the Path-Five mystic sees them as more than a good idea. They are the single most important pursuit in life. In Judaism, the *tsaddik,* or righteous person, is a Path-Five mystic who follows discipline and ethics to union with the divine. Beyond the Ten Commandments there are hundreds of specific rules for living spelled out in the Torah. These rules are interpreted further in the Talmud, and extenuating circumstances that require their modification are carefully laid out.

The fourth commandment, remembering the Sabbath Day to keep it holy, for example, means more than knocking off from work and taking a rest. One cannot carry money, use a telephone, write, knit or sew, drive a car, kindle a fire for cooking, clean, or do work of any kind—even tear toilet paper. Instead, the heart turns to God through prayer, song, dance, time with family and friends, spiritual study, and making love if you are married. *The shall nots assume their real importance in making room for the shalls.* But what happens if your child falls out of a tree and needs medical attention? Illness takes precedence, and you can call 911, boil water, put on bandages, or drive to the hospital. The rules are meant to create space to savor life, remember God, and appreciate your blessings—not as rules for their own sake.

To remember the Sabbath Day to keep it holy, then, is a spiritual discipline. What about the tenth commandment, which instructs us not to covet our neighbor's goods? Think about how much advertising is based on creating covetousness, on making us believe that those with certain sneakers, appliances, computers, houses, or clothing are better off than we are? The Path-Five mystic, who takes the commandment not to covet seriously, will not be found writing ads on Madison Avenue, helping to create a jealous, entitled society. It would be against their ethical code. In fact, they may not watch television. How about the ninth commandment, "You shall not bear false witness against your neighbor." Path-Five mystics won't be found working for the *National Enquirer*, or even reading it. In fact, they will absolutely refuse to talk about another person behind their back. In almost all traditions, disciplining oneself not to gossip is considered a basic step toward spirituality.

In the Hindu tradition, *ahimsa,* or harmlessness, is a basic commandment. And if you take a solemn vow not to harm any living creature, you need the discipline to be a vegetarian. A commitment to harmlessness also extends to your personal health. Alcohol, tobacco, or a diet high in sugar or fat is harmful. To carry out the vow of harmlessness, you would have to be a vegan, an herbivore who eats no animal products at all. Furthermore, since commercial farming involves harm to the environment through pesticide and fertilizer use, you would have to eat only organic foods. Adhering to any code of ethics with the whole heart and mind requires discipline, and discipline develops a strong will.

Will and Intention

Will, a fifth-chakra attribute, is a type of energy that we can compare to the engine of a car. Until the engine is turned on, the car won't go anywhere. Depressed people, for example, have trouble mobilizing will and getting things done. Even getting out of bed in the morning can be a chore. Furthermore, when we are depressed, we are likely to be confused and aimless, doing a little bit of this and a little bit of that, scattering whatever energy we can mobilize.

In order to focus energy, we need intention. Intention is like the steering wheel on a car, determining the direction in which we will move. In addition, intention works like a magnifying glass that catches the sun's rays and focuses them into a beam powerful enough to start a fire. When will and intention are developed through living a disciplined life, according to rules that we consider a divine template for right living, tremendous personal power results. Great acts of compassion, creativity, healing, and service can be accomplished through the path of discipline. The Hindus call these powers *siddhis*, the

Christians, *charisms*. They include such gifts as prophecy, healing, bilocation, mind reading, and the ability to levitate or walk on water. Jesus, in fact, was one of the best known Path-Five mystics. He was true to God and his moral beliefs in every way. And he avoided the pitfalls of Path Five because all his teachings were based on kindness and love.

St. Paul started out as an unhealed zealot drawn to the fifth path. He was self-righteously on his way to kill Christians when he had his conversion experience and healing by Jesus. He sums up the need for love and compassion in his powerful letter to the Corinthians:

> If I speak in the tongues of men and of angels, but have not love, I am a noisy gong or a clanging cymbal. And if I have prophetic powers, and understand all mysteries and all knowledge, and if I have all faith, so as to remove mountains, but have not love, I am nothing. If I give away all I have, and if I deliver my body to be burned, but have not love, I gain nothing."[2]

Paul defined love as patient and kind, never rude, boastful, or arrogant. It doesn't insist on its own way, nor is it resentful or angry. Furthermore, he pointed out that love is perfect and never ends, while prophecy or knowledge or speaking in tongues are imperfect and impermanent. He writes, "When I was a child, I spoke like a child, I thought like a child, I reasoned like a child; when I became a man, I gave up childish things."[3] The Path-Five mystic is a grown-up who knows that love is the foundation upon which discipline stands, and that any act or belief that is unloving has to do with human will, not Divine Will.

Suggestions for the Path-Five Mystic

1. Reflect on love. When you are feeling zealous or righteous about anything, reflect on whether you are doing God's Will, your own, or someone else's. Ask the question, "Is my belief or action respectful and kind, or is it based in anger or judgment?" If the latter is true, pursue the personal healing required to give up the childish things that St. Paul spoke about. If you are a member of a group whose beliefs are based on fear and judgment, rather than on respect or love, extricate yourself.

2. Act with integrity. *Integrity* means "wholeness." Actions are whole when they conform to inner beliefs. If you believe in harmlessness, be a vegetarian. If you believe that abortion is murder, avoid actions that lead to pregnancy. If you believe in the Sabbath, keep it holy. If you believe that slandering others is wrong, don't gossip. The tension that results when actions and beliefs are out of accord leads to anxiety, depression, and loss of will.

3. Study the Ten Commandments as well as the remainder of the Book of Exodus. Do you, in fact, keep the commandments? Go through each one carefully, writing down your reflections on each one. What would it personally mean to you to keep them wholeheartedly? Are you willing to make the intention to do so? Then continue through the rest of the Book of Exodus, which spells out a specific code of justice. Reflect on each item. Is it relevant to modern life? Do you subscribe to it? If so, make the intention to bring it into your daily life.

4. Study the precepts of a religion with which you are not familiar. For example, Tibetan Buddhism lists 28 categories of yogic precepts, including such things as the ten causes of regret, the ten things to be done, the ten things one must know, the ten things to be practiced, the ten incentives, the ten things to be persevered in, the ten errors, the fifteen weaknesses, the twelve indispensable things, the ten signs of a superior person, and the ten useless things.[4] Write down the precepts that relate to, and reinforce, the Ten Commandments. Write down other precepts that you find valuable. If you are so moved, form the intention to follow these precepts in your life.

5. Do not judge other people's path or lack of a path. The zealous outlook of Path-Five mystics can easily degenerate into the belief that your way is the only way to God. So what if your friend doesn't meditate. Maybe they don't need to, or perhaps they have other ways of learning to be still and mindful. So what if another friend is holding a grudge. We all work through resentment at our own pace. So what if the disciplines you practice have changed your life and brought you closer to God, but others seem uninterested in following your advice that they do likewise. Remember that there are six other paths to God, with infinite variations on each one. Preaching and proselytizing in order to save others is disrespectful unless they have asked. The slogan "Live and let live" is a wise one.

6. When you are wrong, promptly admit it. This is part of the tenth step of Alcoholics Anonymous and the other Twelve Step programs. Since self-righteousness is a pitfall of the fifth path, you can minimize it by staying scrupulously aware of your actions and words. Let's say that you are writing a report for work at home one evening and that you are tired and stressed. Your husband wants to talk and keeps interrupting. You are feeling increasingly more irritated and self-important, and you finally blow up and say something short or unkind. Promptly admit that you were wrong, listen to your husband, and then ask nicely to be left alone until you have finished.

7. Do an active, fun activity daily. Your wonderful capacity for discipline can also breed rigidity and compulsiveness. Refresh yourself on a regular basis by doing something *active* that is fun, if your physical condition allows it. Crossword puzzles may be a diversion, but playing Frisbee, taking a hike, riding a bike, making love, dancing wildly in the living room, or watching the stars from your roof are much more effective at getting you out of your head and into your body.

✲ CHAPTER SEVEN

Path Six
Opening the Wisdom Eye

Contemplation and Transformation

Twenty-five hundred years ago, in the North of India, there lived a prince named Gautama Siddhartha. His parents went to inordinate lengths to shield him from suffering, and he grew up surrounded with opulence and every sense pleasure. Married to a beautiful cousin at 16, Siddhartha soon had a young son and all the material possessions a person could desire. But his soul was restless, empty, yearning to know more of life. His greatest desire was to see the world outside the perfumed palace gardens. So one morning, he commanded his charioteer to take him into the city. Despite the king's instructions that Siddhartha be shown only things of beauty, he soon saw four sights that changed his life.

The first sight was a very old man. Since the prince had never seen an elderly person before, he was shocked by the realization that the human body eventually withers. The second sight was a sick person, and suddenly the prince knew that the human body is unreliable. One can be young and vigorous at one moment and struck down by illness the next. The third sight was a corpse on its way to the burning grounds for cremation. When the charioteer told him that all people eventually die, the prince was aghast. Life was not only full of changes, but undependable and impermanent, with death the only certainty. The fourth sight was a *sadhu*, a holy man, so poor that he possessed only a begging bowl and a walking stick. Despite his poverty, the sadhu's face shown with inner peace. Surely he had an answer to the question of why people suffer, and he had found some way out of that suffering.

That very night, the legend goes, the young prince fled the palace and took up the life of an aspiring sadhu. He studied with various teachers, but finding their knowledge insufficient to explain human suffering, he began to practice severe austerities. Near death from fasting, Siddhartha realized that self-torture was not the way to enlightenment. Eventually he found his way to the town of Bohd Gaya and circled a bodhi tree seven times. He sat down to meditate, vowing not to rise until he was enlightened and had perceived the truth about human existence and the end of suffering.

On the night of the full moon in May, Siddhartha attained enlightenment by realizing four noble truths: (1) life inevitably involves suffering; (2) attachments and aversions—our cravings to have some things and avoid others—create suffering; (3) the end to suffering is reached through renouncing these cravings; and (4) the way to nonattachment (renouncement) is attained by practice of the *dharma,* an eight-fold way of right thinking, meditating, and living that develops compassion and knowledge of one's own true nature.

Siddhartha's spiritual eye, the sixth chakra, was opened, and he was thereafter called the Buddha, or the Awakened One. He remained in a state of deep meditation for seven times seven days after his awakening before he arose from his deep *samadhi,* or state of union, and began his life as a teacher.

A Buddha is not a god, but a mortal who, after confronting the emptiness of material life, dies to the ego or small self and is reborn to the bliss of the larger Self— what Buddhists sometimes call "big mind." The Path-Six mystic, like the Buddha, must often reach a point of darkness, a spiritual crisis that causes him to die to his prior life in order to awaken to a new reality of peace, compassion, and divine union. And like the Buddha, such individuals are motivated to a life of contemplation and meditation although they may still function in the secular world.

Death and Rebirth

The sixth path is the direction *West* on the Medicine Wheel. This is the place of mystery, where the sun sets and we descend into darkness, alone with ourselves. Not only mystics, but every person, will eventually experience the fertile mystery of darkness. The day that we are diagnosed with a life-challenging illness, for example, we die to who we thought we were and enter a period of darkness and potential transformation. This is a kind of ego death during which our previous identity no longer serves us, and we enter a time of unknowing. The ground quakes beneath our feet, and our previous assumptions and behaviors fail to provide stability. We ask questions such as: "Who am I?" "What is the meaning of life?" and "What is a life well lived?" The sacred space between the death of the old and the birth of the new is what the 15th-century Christian mystic, St. John of the Cross, called "the dark night of the soul." The suffering we endure is a powerful motivator to ask the kind of spiritual questions that the Buddha did— questions that may not occur to us when life is running smoothly.

A period of wandering in the wilderness, replete with trials and tribulations, is common to the spiritual stories of many traditions. The Israelites wandered for 40 years after the end of their bondage in Egypt before they finally entered the "promised land." Jesus spent 40 days in the wilderness, tempted by the devil, before he began to teach.

If we are willing to view the dark night of the soul as a spiritual opportunity, an initiation into a new life, we can awaken to a new reality. While very few people attain a state of permanent Self-realization or God-Union, dark nights can be great awakeners of faith, love, compassion, and the recognition that we are more than our bodies.

In my practice as a therapist, I have had the privilege of meeting many people during their dark nights when loss of health, relationships, a job, or other crisis challenges them to be reborn. It has been truly humbling to sit with people and listen to their stories of death and resurrection. Most poignant are the many stories of people with AIDS or advanced cancer who say that they have learned so much through the illness, that if given the choice to return to their previous life and health, they would not take it, even though they realize that their illness is mortal. My book *Fire in the Soul* was inspired by the dark night, and contains many stories of people who faced the mystery and were transformed psychologically and spiritually.

But not all Path-Six mystics are catapulted into a spiritual awakening by crisis, nor do all people who endure crisis end up on a spiritual quest. This path, like each of the others, appeals to natural predilections within the individual. The need to explore the riddle of existence, to overcome suffering, to be of service to others, and the willingness to devote oneself to long periods of meditation, contemplation, and spiritual inquiry are prerequisites for this path. While I enjoy meditation, for example, I don't have a contemplative calling like some of my Christian, Jewish, Hindu, and Buddhist friends do who regularly participate in ten-day, forty-day, hundred day, year-long and even three-year silent meditation retreats.

A Call to the Contemplative Life

Many Catholic monks, nuns, and priests respond to an inner call from God, the Latin name for which is a *vocation.* God calls them to religious life of different sorts, including lives of silent contemplation and prayer. Carmelites, for example, are a cloistered order who have a vocation of praying for the world. The Christian contemplative tradition stems from the second-century desert fathers who lived in remote caves and tents, dedicating their lives to prayer, meditation, and frequent fasting to thin the veil between this reality and an expanded state of consciousness in which they could realize their essential unity with God. Their predecessors were the Essenes, a Jewish sect that existed at the time of Jesus, and with whom he may have spent considerable time in his early years.

The archetype of the wiseman or wisewoman on the mountaintop, or in the cave, to whom people make spiritual pilgrimages, fits the Path-Six mystic. Ramana Maharshi is one of the most venerated saints of India in modern times, and many took the pilgrimage to be in his presence. Born near Madras in 1879, he was captivated by mysticism since childhood, and naturally inquired into the mysteries of life. At 17, he had a powerful experience in the home of his uncle. Suddenly, and without warning, he swooned and dropped to the floor. He felt his lifeforce ebb away and began to grow stiff and cold, as if he were dying. He noted that his consciousness, the sense of "I," was still present independent of his body, and he began to think, *Who am I?*

Through this process of self-inquiry, he deduced that he could not be the body, because it decays, nor the intellect, because the brain also perishes with death. He could not be his actions or emotions, for these, too, were impermanent. He had a full-blown, vivid realization that he was the "deathless Spirit" that transcended the body, the innermost Self that is one with God. From that moment on, he spent every waking hour absorbed in the Self, in a state of *samadhi*, or blissful God-Union.

While many people have a temporary realization of the Self, for Ramana Maharshi it was permanent. The ego, with its attachments and aversions, never again clouded over the spiritual sun within his heart. Within a few weeks of his realization, he left home and went to Mount Arunchala, sacred to the god Shiva. He sat in a pit for years, absorbed in blissful meditation, totally unaware of the ants who bit him and the welts that covered his body; impervious to hunger or cold. He made no effort to sustain his life, so people fed him until gradually he began to return to the world and teach those who sought him out. Like the Buddha, he received enlightenment through direct experience, rather than through prescribed teachings and disciplines.

The Practice of Self-Inquiry and Mindfulness

Unlike the Path-Five mystic who follows rules and disciplines handed down from others, the Path-Six mystic relies on direct experience. Ramana Maharshi used his experience of death and the question, "Who am I?" to formulate a path of self-inquiry both as a form of meditation and in daily life. This practice weakens the ego's claim to specialness and its addiction to getting what it likes and avoiding what it doesn't like. When something good or bad happens, he counseled, when you experience either triumph or tragedy, ask to whom this is happening. Eventually you will have the realization that the entire experience is illusory, a kind of play, and that the real Self is unaffected by the drama.

The Maharshi, as he was called, taught very little verbally. His main teaching tool was Spiritual Silence, through which he transmitted his state of being to others. He believed profoundly in meditation, since self-inquiry can only be successful for those who have learned to keep the mind still. He suggested practicing breath control, a basic form of meditation, as a way to quiet the chattering mind. And indeed, belly breathing is the foundation of stress reduction and anxiety control taught in modern medical clinics.

The Buddha, too, taught a form of self-inquiry that is practiced by many people today in medical settings. It is called insight or mindfulness meditation, and once again, the starting point is the breath. Rather than controlling the breath, it is simply watched, every nuance of its coming in and going out the focus of attention. Nothing is judged as good or bad, only the quality of awareness matters. Next, attention is expanded to the body, and physical sensations are noticed. Pleasure is no different than pain, for again, awareness is the only goal. When emotions are experienced, the meditator again takes the stance of nonattachment. Joy or anxiety are equal. When sounds are heard, there is no difference between a Bach concerto or a jackhammer. Both are simply sense perceptions. When attention wanders and thinking takes over, the meditator catches herself and returns to the breath, gradually expanding awareness out again as the mind quiets.

Gradually, over time, insight is gained about the transitory nature of all phenomena and the way that the ego avoids pain and courts pleasure. Are you angry? The normal tendency of the mind is to blame someone or something outside yourself. But through insight meditation, one realizes that you yourself, your own ego with its judgments, is the source of the anger. The practice leads to a kind of spacious awareness called "witness consciousness." Good or bad events in daily life are taken less personally, and they are also observed as transient phenomena. Furthermore, one learns how to pay attention, how to be present, which invites holy moments and makes life much more enjoyable. This skill is called mindfulness, or moment-by-moment attention. Imagine eating your favorite meal mindfully, savoring the aroma, textures, and tastes. Now imagine eating the same thing mindlessly while watching television, having a conversation, or reading the newspaper. Much of the richness of the experience is lost. To be awake, then, is to be mindful.

Mindfulness meditation can benefit almost anyone, as demonstrated by Jon Kabat-Zinn, Ph.D., whose well-known center for stress reduction and relaxation at the University of Massachusetts Medical School is a program of his Center for Mindfulness in Medicine. His bestselling book, *Full Catastrophe Living*, is a portable version of the stress-reduction program and a testimony to how mindfulness can help people live creatively and peacefully with pain, chronic illness, and other adversities. The program is offered not only for patients at the medical school, but also for people in prisons and in the inner city. Participants develop mindfulness and stress hardiness, as well as deep compassion for themselves and others. Once again, the bottom line of spiritual awakening is kindness and love.

Centering and Contemplative Prayer

Both self-inquiry and mindfulness meditation are

active processes that use the mind to inquire into its own nature. This, as we have discussed, is a helpful process for most people. But ultimately, in order to reach Self-realization or God-Union, the mind cannot dissect itself. It has to transcend itself. In other words, you can take the train to meet your lover, but you have to get off to run into her arms.

Father Thomas Keating of the Snowmass Monastery in Colorado, whom I mentioned earlier in this book, is a contemplative Trappist monk who teaches a type of meditation called "centering prayer," the intention of which is to run into the arms of the Divine Beloved, to enter into a relationship with God. Centering prayer is the first step in an evolving process that may ultimately lead to contemplative prayer, the gift of God-Union that comes through grace. In his excellent book *Open Mind, Open Heart,* Keating begins by listing what contemplative prayer is not.

First, it is not a relaxation exercise, although relaxation may be a side effect. Second, it is not a charismatic gift like speaking in tongues, being slain in the spirit, or levitating. In fact, such gifts may have little to do with holiness and can create a kind of egotism, a spiritual materialism. Third, contemplative prayer is not a parapsychological phenomenon like ESP or an out-of-body experience. Fourth, it is not a mystical phenomenon like ecstasy, visions, or God talking to you. Furthermore, it is impossible to judge the fruits of centering prayer during a meditation session. Changes occur in the unconscious mind, until one day, when walking down the supermarket aisle, you may finally experience the transformation of God-Union. As such, the preparatory process of centering prayer is an act of pure faith, totally unlike mindfulness meditation, in which the practitioner is engaging in a conscious process of awakening.

At its most practical level, Keating defines centering prayer as the consent to God's presence and action in our lives. There is no petitioning, praising, or whining in this type of prayer. It is a simple descent into silence, a resting in God, beyond thought. But laying aside thoughts is no simple task, since the nature of the mind is to think, compare, and evaluate. When you find yourself doing this during centering prayer, you gently introduce a prayer word, repeating it over and over until the mind quiets again. The repetition of the prayer word has only one goal: to remind you of your intention to let go and rest in God, thus opening you to a level of spiritual awareness deeper than the thinking mind.

Thoughts, according to Keating, are like boats floating down a river. We are so identified with the thoughts, that we don't notice the river they are floating upon. That river, which is not apparent in everyday consciousness, is our "participation in God's being." As we learn to be silent, and spaces appear between thoughts, the river becomes visible.

Those of us who have the passion to immerse ourselves in meditation with the intention to awaken to God's presence are walking the sixth path. Will we succeed in this lifetime? According to Keating, we may never know, since the experience of God's radiant presence remains hidden for the majority of us. He quotes Ruth Burroughs, a Carmelite nun, who distinguishes between *lights on* mysticism and *lights off* mysticism. In the latter case, God-Union is happening at a soul level, beyond our perception. You notice it not in meditation, but in the transformation of your life. Peace, compassion, equanimity, mindfulness, charity, and love are the fruits of union, whether hidden or perceived.

Suggestions for the Path-Six Mystic

1. Adopt a regular meditation practice that suits your temperament and religious tradition. Christians may enjoy Keating's instructions for centering prayer, and centering prayer groups exist in many cities. Jews, too, have a contemplative tradition that is beautifully presented in Aryeh Kaplan's book, *Jewish Meditation*. Hindu and Buddhist texts on meditation abound, as do practice groups. Beginners often confuse meditation with guided visualization. While the latter is very useful in many contexts, it is different from meditation, whose purpose is to let of thoughts and images. In fact, if Jesus or the Buddha appear in your meditation, or if God speaks to you, the instructions are to pay no attention and go back to your breath, your mantra, or your prayer world. At least 20 minutes of your chosen meditation twice a day is recommended by almost all teachers.

2. Find a teacher. A deep meditation practice requires guidance from those familiar with the experience. They need not be enlightened, but if they are, they are not likely to talk about it. Beware of teachers who are flashy, make extravagant claims, or ask for large sums of money. Beware of teachers who treat you like someone special or suggest that having sex with them will hasten your journey to awakening. Many examples of the latter have occurred in recent years, often with great damage to the individuals and organizations involved.

3. If possible, meditate and study with a group. The companionship of like-minded individuals stimulates practice, understanding, and spiritual growth. Buddhists, for example, "take refuge"— which means making a spiritual commitment to making these things central to your life—in the Buddha, in the Dharma or the path to enlightenment, and in the Sangha, the spiritual community of those who walk the same path.

4. Go on regular retreats. Concentrated periods of meditation are recommended in all traditions, and aspiring Path-Six mystics often go on week-long (or even longer) retreats as often as their schedules permit. *But please note* *that intensive meditation is not safe for all people.* It dismantles the ego, and in those who are depressed or who have a shaky sense of self, psychotic breaks can result. Most conscientious teachers prescreen applicants for long retreats in order to minimize these dangers, but you have to take responsibility for yourself. If you have a history of mental illness, poor self-esteem, depression, or are in crisis, long retreats are not recommended.

5. Be gentle with yourself. The tendency to judge your progress and find yourself lacking is a pitfall on the path. After 25 years of meditation, most of the time I am busy bringing my mind back from thinking. The only definition of a good meditation is one that you sat down and did. Remember Keating's idea that transformation is often an unconscious process. The results you see in your life— increased peace, compassion, and equanimity—may be the only visible fruits of practice.

6. Study the lives of the mystics from various traditions. Can you identify their paths to God? Remember that aspects of many different paths supplement one's primary path. Ramana Maharshi was primarily an experiential Path-Six mystic, but he also had the devotional qualities of Path Four, and adhered to precepts of living from Path Five. There is a lot to be learned from reading about the inner lives, the thoughts, and experiences of saints and mystics, as well as about the technical aspects of their practices. As in Zen stories in which the master utters a simple phrase and the student suddenly moves to enlightenment, sometimes a story or a metaphor can cause startling insights and revelations to crystallize, seemingly out of nowhere.

7. Steer clear of *spiritual materialism.* This term was coined by the late Tibetan Buddhist, Chögyam Trungpa Rinpoche. As the powers of concentration deepen, siddhis and charisms often result. You may become aware of what other people are thinking, have precognitive dreams or intuitions about future events, receive visions or teachings in dreams, be able to leave your body, or like the Hindu saint Sai Baba, develop the capacity to bilocate. Attachment to these powers is dangerous because they can feed the ego and distract you from the goal of God-Union.

※　　※　　※

❈ CHAPTER EIGHT

Path Seven
The Way of Faith
Paradox and Grace

Once upon a time, in Ancient China, there lived a Taoist farmer who followed the Great Way to God. He was considered a wealthy man because he had a horse to help with plowing. One early spring morning, his horse ran off. When the villagers heard, they hastened to his home to express their sympathy. "What a terrible thing," they lamented. But all the Taoist farmer said was, "Maybe."

The next morning, his horse returned, leading an entire herd of wild mustangs. The townspeople rushed over, exclaiming at his good fortune. "Now you are the richest man in the province," they exalted. But all the farmer said was, "Maybe." The following morning the farmer's only son awoke at dawn to begin breaking one of the wild horses. It promptly threw him, and his leg was broken. The townspeople rushed over in alarm. "What a terrible thing," they wept. "Without the help of your only son, how can you plant your fields?" But all the farmer said was, "Maybe."

The next afternoon, the emperor's soldiers rode into town, kicking up an enormous cloud of dust. They had come to conscript all the young men into war, but the farmer's son could not go because of his broken leg. The townspeople once again gathered around to marvel at the farmer's good luck. But all he said was, "Maybe."

The story continues in the same fashion for many more verses, illustrating the important principle of nonattachment and its relationship to faith. The farmer knows that the Tao is harmonious and just, that all things conspire creatively for life to grow and evolve. Incidents that appear either good or bad can never be judged in isolation. Life is a paradox in which all things are relative and interrelated. One can only have faith in the ultimate working of the Tao.

Faith

As the Buddha pointed out in the Four Noble Truths, suffering is an inevitable part of life unless one develops a steadfast attitude of nonattachment. But in our society, the failure to be swayed by praise and blame or tragedy and triumph is often misconstrued as heartlessness, lack of interest, depression, or psychological isolation. And indeed, it can be. In order to distinguish nonattachment based on faith from depression or closed-heartedness, one must again look to the fruits of spirit in a person's life. Are they kind, helpful, creative, loving, and compassionate? These are the indications of faith and the willingness not to demean God as a petty tyrant who rewards and punishes.

It is easy to have faith in God, in the Tao, when things are going well. But faith is put to the test in times of hardship and crisis. Then the spiritual growth that has developed from following any of the paths is called into action. Path Seven, the Way of Faith, is like a river fed by the other streams. Once developed, however, it becomes a path unto itself, and those who walk it become lights unto the world—like Mother Teresa or Mahatma Gandhi.

St. Paul defined faith as the substance of things hoped for but not seen. Most of us hope that the Universe is loving, but it takes faith to maintain that hope in the face of the tragedies that occur daily. How can rape, murder, war, and illness be loving acts? And yet, in speaking to those who have had near-death experiences and deathbed visions in which they rise out of the myopia of daily life, we are told that all events happen for the greater good, that nothing is accidental or without the capacity to spur our evolution as loving co-creators with God.

A patient of mine named Paul was once hospitalized on Christmas Eve, being fed intravenously, since a chronic bowel disease had caused him to lose significant weight. A devout Catholic with no knowledge of the chakras, yoga, or the energy body, he felt a sudden burst of energy that began at the base of his spine and rose up like fire through his body to the crown of his head. Suddenly, Paul's entire view of the world changed. Everything seemed perfect, working as it should. The nurse walked by with a cart of medications, and he perceived the incredible interrelatedness of all the events that led to the medicines' existence, and the perfect way that they suited each patient. Everything seemed in harmony, beautiful, and working toward the highest good.

When Paul tried to explain this experience to the social worker in his room, she panicked and called for a psychiatrist. The psychiatrist, who had no knowledge of the *kundalini*—the coiled energy that lies at the base of the spine that can suddenly rise to the crown chakra and bring enlightenment—offered my patient Valium. He considered the experience of perfection a temporary psychotic state perhaps due to electrolyte imbalance. Paul refused the Valium and received a great teaching through grace. For the remainder of the night, he would be in the blissful state of Divine union where all things seemed perfect at one moment, and then his mind would seize upon some negative thought or memory. As soon as he began to think fearfully, he would exit the state of Divine union. The ego, the small isolated self with its attachments and aversions, would take over, and he would become its prisoner. But as soon as Paul could let go of these thoughts, his heart and mind would open again and he would enter the state of bliss.

Although the experiences of God-Union faded by

morning, what a wonderful teaching this young man received. When we close down in fear, the lifeforce energy cannot rise and bring us into the direct experience of God. Paul was a Path-Four mystic, devoted to Jesus and his teachings, and he attended Mass most mornings. While it is tempting to explain his experience as a result of his devotion, many devoted people don't have union experiences. They are always a gift of grace. While we can prepare ourselves to receive them, it is not possible to storm the gates of heaven.

If we had to make the journey to God-realization under our own steam, it would not be possible. The mind and the ego are difficult to subdue, and we are only human, so we constantly make mistakes. But just as loving parents give children what they need—not because they have earned it, but because they are loved—God aids *all* her children. And as in the story of the Taoist farmer, we can't dictate the way in which grace arrives, or even what it is. Is winning the lottery a grace if it diverts us from pursuing work that develops our creativity? Isn't addiction a grace when it causes us to hit bottom, undergo an ego death, and learn to trust (as in the First Step of Twelve Step programs) that a power greater than ourselves can help return us to sanity?

The Stages of Faith

Harvard theologian James Fowler published a penetrating study of how we develop faith, and its relationship to our psychological development, which he published in a book entitled *Stages of Faith*. Studies show that we invent God in our own image, or more precisely, in the image of our parents. If our parents were abusive, unreliable, or critical, we are likely to grow up with low self-esteem and imagine a God who is punitive and petty like our parents were. If our parents were loving, we are likely to grow up with high self-esteem and imagine a God, who like our parents, is beneficent, compassionate, and encouraging. As we mature psychologically over the lifespan, and heal wounds to our sense of self, our idea of God—and thus our faith—undergoes systematic changes.

Fowler distinguishes six stages of psychospiritual growth in relation to faith. Small children under the age of seven live in an imaginative world populated by angels and demons, fairies and monsters. Furthermore, they imitate and assume the beliefs of the people around them. So, if a child lives in a frightening household, or is exposed to fire-and-brimstone images of a terrifying God, these images become deeply imbedded in their psyche and can create a fear-based faith. Some fundamentalist preachers, for example, who live in fear of the wrath of God, are still imprisoned by the neurological traces left from an abusive childhood.

From seven until puberty, children undergo a second stage of psychological development in which they tend to divide things into distinct, linear categories: black and white, good and evil, just and unjust. Stories, myths, and drama are interpreted literally, and the child demands reciprocity—an eye for an eye and a tooth for a tooth. The faith of this stage rests in the concept of fairness. But life is not linear, and it seems decidedly unfair if you expect to be rewarded by a Santa Claus God for being good, and punished for being bad—and you don't get what you expect. If, as adults, we are unable to appreciate paradox and relativity like the Taoist farmer, we need to do some healing in order to grow out of the childish concept of reward and punishment into the next stages of faith.

At puberty, children enter a third developmental phase and begin to think for themselves, looking beyond the beliefs of their family. Faith becomes an extension of interpersonal relationships and the need to be acceptable and fit in, conforming to the judgments of one's peer group. According to Fowler, many people remain in this conventional stage of faith, never stepping outside their assumptions to reflect on them. In my experience, dark nights of the soul are valuable because they call unexamined beliefs into question. The person diagnosed with cancer, or the parent whose child is killed, is likely to ask why. In a loving universe, why do bad things happen to good people? The dark night puts us face to face with our most deeply held beliefs and offers the opportunity to examine and revise those beliefs, arriving at a new level of faith.

As life progresses from adolescence to adulthood, or after we have survived a dark night of the soul that moves us beyond the third stage of faith, a fourth stage unfolds. We develop the capacity to reflect on ourselves as individuals and face the inevitable tensions between who we are and what people want us to be; between what we believe and what they want us to believe; between meeting our own needs and being of service to others. Ultimately, we become disillusioned with previous linear ideas about God and begin to seek more multileveled approaches to faith.

By midlife, says Fowler, we have known the "sacrament of defeat." Life is not easy, and there are no simple prescriptions for happiness. It is clear that God does not reward the just and punish the unjust. We are aware of the paradoxes that life holds; we are simultaneously alone and all one; we can perceive powerful truths and at the same time appreciate their relativity. Stories and myths reach us metaphorically, through the language of Spirit. But there is still tension in this fifth stage of faith. We live caught between "an untransformed world and a transforming vision."[1]

The sixth stage of faith is what Fowler calls universalizing faith, and he considers it relatively rare. It is the faith of the Taoist farmer, of the true mystic who perceives the larger Whole that is greater than the sum of its parts. People at this stage may act in strange and unconventional ways, and are often considered subversive of religious structures. Like Jesus or St. Joan of Arc, they may be such a threat to those structures that they are martyred, only to be venerated in death as they were feared in life. Fowler cites figures like Gandhi, Martin Luther King, Mother Teresa, Dag Hammarskjöld, the rabbi Abraham Heschel, and the Catholic priest Thomas Merton as examples of universalizing faith.

The nature of life is a process of evolution in which we become progressively more whole, psychologically and spiritually. Our faith is a measure of that evolution, whether we are Jews or Christians, Hindus or Buddhists, Moslems, Taoists, Native Americans, or free spirits who adhere to no particular tradition. Every religion and system for growth has its own teaching stories and precepts for living. When we reach the level of universalizing faith, we can see the beauty in all traditions and appreciate the way in which the various paths lend themselves to people of different types, no matter what their tradition may be.

In 1871, the great Lakota visionary and warrior Crazy Horse saw a future time of peace—after two world wars—when people of all colors and beliefs would be united under a great sacred tree. Once again the earth would be honored and life appreciated as a gift from the Creator. The tree of life is an enduring symbol, common to many cultures. Its roots are in the ground, and its different branches touch the sky. Beneath this tree of shelter, people find respect, tolerance, charity, compassion, unity, and love. If you are on the mystic path, you are a representative of a branch of the sacred peace tree. Together we can bring a new world, a time of heaven on earth into being.

There are no specific suggestions for the Path-Seven

mystic, because the Way of Faith is the trunk of the tree, which grows together with its branches. Whatever your primary and secondary paths may be, follow them with all your mind, heart, and soul. For you are the hope of the world. No one ever develops faith and comes into relationship with God without touching the lives of others and becoming a force for good. Like a stone tossed in a pond, the ripples of every prayer, every meditation, every discipline, every loving act spread through the universe for the benefit of all beings.

May more and more of us awaken to God in these chaotic times, pregnant with both danger and opportunity. May we live the words of the Christian mystic Meister Eckhart who wrote, "The eye with which I see God is the same eye as that with which he sees me. My eye and the eye of God are one eye, one vision, one knowledge, and one love."[2] For this is the vision that unites all seven paths and creates the rainbow bridge to a new earth and a new heaven.

❊ NOTES

Introduction

1. New Testament, Acts 9: 5.

2. *The Upanishads*, translation by Swami Prabhavananda and Frederick Manchester, Sri Ramakrishna Math, Weldun Press, Madras, India, p. 35, 1968.

3. *Tao Te Ching*, translated by Stephen Mitchell, Harper Perennial, San Francisco, p. 70, 1988.

4. *Tibetan Yoga and Secret Doctrines*, W. Y. Evans-Wentz, Oxford University Press, New York, p. 71, 1958.

5. *Noble Red Man: Lakota Wisdomkeeper, Mathew King,* Harvey Arden, Beyond Words Publishing, Inc., Hillsboro, OR, p. 13, 1994.

6. *Unseen Rain: Quatrains of Rumi,* by John Moyne and Coleman Barks, Threshold Books, Putney, VT, p. 83, 1986.

Chapter One

1. *The Mystery of Numbers*, Rosemarie Schimmel, Oxford University Press, New York, London, 1993.

2. *Pranayama*, Swami Kuvalayananda, Kaivalyadhams, Lonavla, India, 1966.

3. The words of Jesus, Luke 11:34, revised standard Bible. Please note that all subsequent citations from the Bible are from the revised standard edition.

4. Personal communication from Dik Darnell, trained in the Lakota medicine ways by the late ceremonial Chief Frank Fools Crow.

Chapter Two

1. William Arrowsmith, *My Words Are Like the Stars*, adapted from Chief Seattle's speech as recorded by Dr. Henry B. Smith, from *How Can One Sell the Air?: Chief Seattle's Vision,* edited by Eli Gifford and R. Michael Cook, The Book Publishing Company, Summertown, TN, p. 75, 1992.

2. Mathew King, from *Noble Red Man: Lakota Wisdomkeeper Mathew King*, compiled and edited by Harvey Arden, Beyond Words Publishing, Inc., Hillsboro, OR, 1994.

3. Charles Alexander Eastman, *The Soul of the Indian*, Houghton Mifflin, Boston, p. 5, 1911.

4. Ibid., title page.

Chapter Three

1. Anthony DeMello.

2. The words of Jesus, Matthew 6: 19-21.

Chapter Five

1. Adapted from a teaching story of Anthony de Mello, in *Taking Flight*, Image Books, Doubleday, New York, 1990.

2. Mother Teresa, *No Greater Love,* New World Library, Novato, CA, p. 85, 1997.

3. Christoper Isherwood, *Ramakrishna and His Disciples,* Vedanta Press, Hollywood, CA, p. 321, 1965.

4. Cited by Matthew Fox, *Original Blessing: A Primer in Creation Spirituality*, Bear and Co., Santa Fe, NM, p. 132, 1983.

Chapter Six

1. The code of justice given on Sinai is found just after the Ten Commandments in Exodus, occupying the entire remainder of this book.

2. 1 Corinthians 13:1-3.

3. 1 Corinthians 13: 11.

4. The Precepts of the Gurus can be found in *Tibetan Yoga and Secret Doctrines*, edited by W.Y. Evans-Wentz, Oxford University Press, London, pp. 67-100, 958.

Chapter Eight

1. James W. Fowler, *Stages of Faith: The Psychology of Human Development and the Quest for Meaning*. Viking Press, New York, p. 198, 1981.

2. Cited by Andrew Harvey and Anne Baring in *The Mystic Vision: Daily Encounters with the Divine*, Harper San Francisco, p. 95, 1995.

✳ ABOUT THE AUTHOR

Joan Borysenko, Ph.D., has been described as a respected scientist, gifted therapist, and unabashed mystic. Trained at Harvard Medical School, where she was an instructor in medicine until 1988, she is a pioneer in mind/body medicine, women's health, and the author of several books, including the bestselling *Minding the Body, Mending the Mind; The Power of the Mind to Heal;* and *A Woman's Book of Life.*

※   ※   ※

We hope you enjoyed this Hay House book.
If you would like to receive a free catalog
featuring additional Hay House books and products,
or if you would like information about the
Hay Foundation, please contact:

Hay House, Inc.
P.O. Box 5100
Carlsbad, CA 92018-5100

(760) 431-7695 or **(800) 654-5126**
(760) 431-6948 (fax) or **(800) 650-5115 (fax)**

Please visit the Hay House Website at:
www.hayhouse.com

※   ※   ※